Life Principles for Spiritual Warfare

Life Principles for

Spiritual Warfare

EDDIE RASNAKE

Advancing the Ministries of the Gospel

AMG Publishers

God's Word to you is our highest calling.

Following God

HOW TO DEVELOP A QUIET TIME

© 2010 by Eddie Rasnake

Published by AMG Publishers. All Rights Reserved.

First Printing, 2010

ISBN 13: 978-0-89957-343-4
ISBN 10: 0-89957-343-6

Edited by Christy Graeber and Rick Steele
Interior Layout by Jennifer Ross and Rick Steele

Cover design by Michael Largent at Indoor Graphics Corporation, Chattanooga, TN
http://www.indoorgraphics.com/

Printed in Canada
18 17 16 15 14 –M– 7 6 5 4 3

Other new releases in the Following God® Series:
Life Principles from Paul's Co-Workers
by Richard Soule

and

Life Principles for Worship
from the Feasts of Israel
by Rick Shepherd

Look for these new Following God® study books in
your local Christian book stores or on our websites:
www.AMGPublishers.com
www.FollowingGod.com

Acknowledgments

I am ever grateful to my dear friends, Wayne Barber and Rick Shepherd, with whom I partnered in the conception of this Bible study series that became Following God. A big "thank you" to the folks at AMG Publishers for their high view of the Word of God and their commitment to quality, accuracy, and depth in all the Bible study resources they produce. I am grateful to partner with a publisher that places the ministry side of writing as more important than the business side. Special kudos to Rick Steele, Christy Graeber, Trevor Overcash, Warren Baker, Dale Anderson, Dan Penwell, and John Fallahee for their help and support. Most of all, I remain grateful to the Lord Jesus, who saved a wretch like me and continues to lead me in what it means to follow Him with a whole heart.

EDDIE RASNAKE

About the Author

Eddie Rasnake met Christ as a freshman in college. He graduated with honors from East Tennessee State University. He and his wife, Michele, served for nearly seven years on the staff of Campus Crusade for Christ. Their first assignment was the University of Virginia, and while there they also started a Campus Crusade ministry at James Madison University. Eddie then served four years as campus director of the Campus Crusade ministry at the University of Tennessee. Eddie has served on the staff of Woodland Park Baptist Church since 1989, where he now ministers as a Senior Associate Pastor. He has been ministering in Eastern Europe in the role of equipping local believers for more than two decades and has published materials in Afrikaans, German, Greek, Italian, Romanian, Russian, and Tegulu. Eddie was a founding board member of the Center for Christian Leadership in Tirana, Albania, and the Bible Training Center in Eleuthera, Bahamas. He also served as chaplain for the Chattanooga Lookouts (Cincinatti Reds AA affiliate) baseball team for seven years. Eddie and his wife Michele have four children and live in Chattanooga, Tennessee.

About the Following God Series

Three authors and fellow ministers, Wayne Barber, Eddie Rasnake, and Rick Shepherd, teamed up in 1998 to write a character-based Bible study for AMG Publishers. Their collaboration developed into the title, *Life Principles from the Old Testament*. Since 1998 these same authors and AMG Publishers have produced five more character-based studies—each consisting of twelve lessons geared around a five-day study of a particular Bible personality. More studies of this type are in the works. In 2001, AMG Publishers launched a different Following God category called the Following God® Discipleship Series. The titles introduced in the Discipleship Series are among the first Following God® studies to be published in a topically-based format (rather than Bible character-based). However, the interactive study format that readers have come to love remains constant with each new Following God® release. As new titles and categories are being planned, our focus remains the same: to provide excellent Bible study materials that point people to God's Word in ways that allow them to apply truths to their own lives. More information on this groundbreaking series can be found on the following web pages:

www.AMGPublishers.com
www.FollowingGod.com

Preface

An incredibly popular subject of discussion in the body of Christ today is the whole area commonly called "Spiritual Warfare." The prominence this subject is afforded is not surprising, and I believe it will become more and more relevant to the Western world in the days ahead. As one reads the Gospel accounts, it doesn't take long to see that there seemed to be much more overt demonic activity in Palestine at the time of Christ than there is in America today. But that is not true of our world as a whole. Even in the west that is changing. Western culture is moving away from secular humanism with its emphasis on rationalism and the mind. The world view growing toward dominance is what some have called "cosmic humanism"—a man-centered belief system with the added dimension of the supernatural. This evolving world view is reflected in the rapid embracing and repackaging of Eastern mystic beliefs into what is called the New Age movement. What many Americans don't see is that behind much of these beliefs is an increased dabbling in the occult and a revival of ancient paganism and witchcraft. As this movement grows, I believe we will see much more overt demonic activity in the west.

What will be the church's response to cosmic humanism? It seems spiritual warfare is being discussed and taught more now than at any time in recent history. Yet, much of what is being taught today about Satan and demons is erroneous and unbiblical. The fruit of much modern teaching is actually spiritual instability instead of maturity. However, I do not perceive this as a completely negative state of affairs. The increased attention given to the subject of spiritual warfare will, I believe, be used of the Lord for good. I expect that it will move all believers to search out the Scriptures and determine what the Word really teaches about Satan and the believer's response to him. Admittedly, there is much imbalance in this arena of theology today. Yet, I fully expect this movement to mature and become more centered on the teaching of Scripture and less on subjective experience. The goal of this book is to become a partner in this process. It is not my heart to throw stones at particular doctrines or people. Rather, it is my prayerful ambition to help believers shape convictions that are Biblical. Even if you do not agree with all that is presented in this book, it will hopefully assist you in searching the Scriptures and drawing your own conclusions before the Lord. May the Lord bless your study.

EDDIE RASNAKE

Table of Contents

1

Understanding Satan

If I were God, I probably would not have created the devil. What about you… would you have dared? When we see the trouble he causes today and the damage he has done throughout history, it would seem foolish to want the devil around. Yet one thought forces me to reconsider. God knows more than I. Think about this reality. The battle we enter in the spiritual realm is not a result of God making a mistake. Because He is omniscient, God knew everything Satan would ever do before He created this fallen angel. He was not taken by surprise; He did not say "oops!" Because our Lord is omnipotent, He can bring Satan's scheming to an end whenever He chooses. Although I don't claim to fully understand it, I must begin any consideration of spiritual warfare by acknowledging that God has a purpose in allowing it to be a possibility. Because of this truth, I have been driven to the revelation of God in hopes of understanding more about this one we call Satan. I invite you to join me in this quest.

As we build our doctrine in any area of the Christian life, we should seek balance. Yet we can look in almost any direction and see imbalance. Perhaps no area is more vulnerable to this danger than the issue of spiritual warfare. Our adversary the devil appears as an angel of light. He loves to encourage imbalance in our view of him, and I don't believe he really cares which direction that imbalance heads as long as it differs from the mind of God. C.S. Lewis identifies this danger in *The Screwtape Letters*:

The devil loves to encourage imbalance in our view of him.

There are two equal and opposite errors into which our race can fall about the devils. One is to disbelieve in their existence. The other is to believe, and to feel an excessive and unhealthy interest in them. They themselves are equally pleased by both errors, and hail a materialist or magician with the same delight.[1]

THE DANGER OF IMBALANCE

When I was about five years old I was attacked by a very large dog as I played in a neighbor's yard. I still have scars from the deep wounds that I received in my arm. Understandably, I still feel nervous when a barking dog runs toward me. But it is a different story when that dog is on a chain. It may startle me when a barking canine comes running at me, but there is security in knowing that very soon there will be a loud "twang" as that dog reaches the end of its leash. No matter how much effort it expends, the dog can do nothing outside of the limits set by its master. Scripture makes it clear that our adversary, the devil, prowls about like a roaring lion, seeking someone to devour. However, he is a lion on a leash, and God holds the end of it. Understanding this reality should radically affect the way we view spiritual warfare and the enemies enlisted by Satan. The Biblical teaching on spiritual warfare isn't extensive, but it isn't unclear.

📖 Read 2 Corinthians 11:14. What do you learn about how the devil represents himself?

_____

_____

_____

Several words in this Scripture offer warnings that we should heed. First, we see that Satan *"disguises"* himself. Whenever we encounter the enemy of our souls, things are not as they appear. The Greek word translated *"disguises"* here is *metaschematizo* and means "to change the outward appearance of something." This makes it clear that there are potential misunderstandings in every encounter with the devil. Our passage indicates he disguises himself *"as an angel of light."* An angel is a "messenger." This one's message may appear to bring light or illumination, but that is an illusion. In reality, it is darkness, not light, that is associated with the dominion of Satan (see Acts 26:18).

How do believers arrive at an imbalanced view of the devil? One way is allowing our eyes to become focused on him instead of the Lord. A.W. Tozer expressed it well when he said, "Our focus is always and only to be the Lord Jesus Christ, and if the devil appears, he appears dimly and on the periphery." In other words, we see as much of the devil as we need to see when our eyes are on Christ. If our eyes shift to center on Satan, we are probably seeing too much. I have come to recognize that when my focus is on the devil, I begin to believe he is greater than God. That is not truth, but it can appear to be so. To have an accurate view of Satan, we must always keep the Lord in focus.

A second way we can arrive at an imbalanced view of the devil is to have reactionary beliefs instead of studied convictions. Allow me to explain. Christians are always finding something to disagree about. Spiritual warfare is one of many hotly debated doctrines in the body of Christ. When Christians disagree, it is all too easy for us to polarize. When we hear a view we believe to be wrong, it is easy to move to the opposite extreme in reaction to that wrong. Thus our views can become equally wrong in the opposite direction. Amid conflicting doctrinal views in the body of Christ, truth is not usually found at one extreme or the other. It lies somewhere in between. It grieves me that, as some have promoted an imbalanced emphasis on the devil, others have reacted by avoiding the subject altogether. A similar problem surfaced among churches in the 1960s and 1970s. The charismatic movement flourished and began emphasizing the Holy Spirit, sometimes to excess. Many conservative churches did not agree with this emphasis. They reacted by not teaching on the Holy Spirit at all for fear of being counted with the charismatics. Instead of balance, the result was a greater imbalance. If we want a complete and healthy view of spiritual warfare, we must not focus on what we believe to be error. Instead, we must look intently at what God's Word teaches.

There is a third way we can arrive at an imbalanced view of the devil. We can err by drawing our conclusions about him from our experience instead of from the clear teaching of Scripture. There is nothing wrong with having an experience, but experience is a very subjective instructor. Unless I interpret my experience in the light of what God says, I am always in danger of drawing wrong conclusions from it. Let me share an example. Some years ago my wife was diagnosed with cancer. If my focus had been on the experience, and the pain, grief, and fear it brought, it would have been easy to doubt God's goodness. But Scripture clearly teaches that God is good and He does good (Psalm 119:68). When my experience and God's Word do not seem to agree, it is my experience that must be reinterpreted, not God's Word. Years have passed since my wife's diagnosis. God has demonstrated His goodness over and over. Although treatment did not produce remission, God chose to heal her. But in the heat of the battle, I had to put my trust in what God says, not in how we felt or what we were experiencing at the time. If I want to have a balanced view of Satan, I must start with what God says, not with what my experience or someone else's says. Let's face it, Satan, the "Father of Lies," will be happy to give me an experience if by it he can deceive me.

📖 Take a look at Jesus' encounter with the devil in Matthew 4:5–7.

🛑 APPLY What do you think about Satan using Scripture to try to get Jesus to do what he wants?

_____

_____

_____

Does Jesus question the validity of the Scriptures Satan quotes?

_____

_____

_____

> "Our focus is always and only to be the Lord Jesus Christ, and if the devil appears, he appears dimly and on the periphery."
>
> A. W. Tozer

_____

_____

_____

In introducing this lesson I pointed out the importance of balance. Just because we quote a Bible verse to support our view, that doesn't necessarily mean we have arrived at truth. Bible verses can be taken out of context and their meaning twisted. Like prisoners of war, if you torture them long enough you can get verses to confess almost anything. In this passage, Satan is taking verses out of context and twisting their meaning to his own purposes. The whole truth is not found in one verse. It is found in balancing all that Scripture has to say about a matter. The more important the issue, the more essential it is that we look at multiple passages of Scripture. Notice that Jesus does not argue with the truth of the verses that Satan quotes. Instead of saying the devil is wrong, Jesus says, *"on the other hand, it is written"* and quotes another relevant verse. He clarifies the truth by balancing it with another passage to prevent taking the point too far.

As we pursue a balanced view of spiritual warfare, we must start with what God says in His Word. God considered spiritual warfare to be important enough to include in Scripture. A key thing to remember, however, is that Scripture spends a lot more time teaching me how to deal with myself and my own sinful desires than it spends talking about how I am to deal with the devil. The main focus of the New Testament is not dealing with the devil, but walking with God. Let's keep that in perspective.

Satan's Limitations

Who are the enemies of the believer? Notice I said enemies, not enemy. If we are to have a biblical view of spiritual warfare, we must recognize the plurality of opponents facing us. While Satan is chief among them, he is not alone. He is joined in this war by his army of demons: those angels who fell with him when he was cast from heaven. And he is aided in this attack by the world system, which has arrayed itself against God. But perhaps the most useful comrade Satan has in this conflict is found in an unlikely place—us. You see, all of Satan's efforts would be meaningless if there were not within each of us desires that run contrary to God. The Bible calls these desires our "flesh."

To understand what spiritual warfare is all about, we must first understand our enemies. And to do that we must look to the Scriptures and see what they have to say about each of these. We will tackle the world and the flesh in the days ahead, but this week we are starting with a look at Satan.

To understand Satan's make-up, we must first recognize where he came from. Look at the verses below and write what you learn and how that relates to Satan.

The "Father of Lies" will be happy to give me an experience if by it he can deceive me.

Understanding Satan

DAY TWO

📖 Colossians 1:16

_____

_____

_____

📖 Ephesians 1:20–22

_____

_____

_____

Colossians 1:16 tells us, *"For by Him [Jesus]* **all** *things were created, both in the heavens and on earth"* (emphasis mine). You see, Satan is a created being. That tells us first of all that he is under God's sovereignty. We must remember that God's actions are always based on His foreknowledge, so He knew Satan would rebel before He created him. Ephesians 1:20–22 teaches us that when God raised Jesus from the dead, He *"seated Him at His right hand in the heavenly places, far above all rule and authority and power and dominion."* It goes on to say that God has *"put all things in subjection under His feet."* Satan truly is a lion on a leash.

We see the reality of God's sovereignty over Satan most clearly illustrated in the book of Job. You are probably familiar with the story of Job and all that Satan did to him, but if you don't look carefully you might miss the Lord behind all of it. Look at the passages from Job listed in the chart and answer the questions that follow.

What do you think these encounters teach about Satan's relationship to God?

> **God's actions are always based on His foreknowledge, so He knew Satan would rebel before He created him.**

Question	Job 1:6-22	Job 2:1-10
Where does Satan encounter the Lord?		
Who brings up Job in the conversation?		
What is Satan's theory on Job's righteousness?		
What is Satan's plan to test it?		
How does God respond to Satan's plan?		
What specific boundaries does God set on Satan's attack?		
What is Satan's attack?		
How does Job respond?		
Who does Job realize is in control of his misfortune?		

Did You Know?

JOB

Although the book of Job appears just before the Psalms, most scholars believe it was the first book of the Bible to be written. Job probably lived during the same general time as Abraham.

First of all, did you notice the occasion for God's conversation with Satan? Satan is coming with all the angels, *"to present himself before the Lord."* Notice who is reporting to whom. God is the one in charge. Second, it is God, not Satan, who brings the whole matter up, and He does it twice. He says, *"Have you considered my servant Job?"* When Satan suggests that Job only serves God because He blesses him, notice what God does: He releases Satan to attack Job, giving him freedom he didn't have before and setting the boundaries for what Satan can and cannot do. In chapter one He allows Satan to touch Job's possessions and children, but not Job himself. In chapter two, when that doesn't cause Job to curse God, God allows Satan to torment Job, but not to kill him. God is in control of the whole process. In fact, no one ever gives Satan credit for doing any of it. Throughout the whole book, Job always says, "God did this." And God agrees. Look at what God says in 2:3, *"you [Satan] incited Me against him, to ruin him without cause."* Even Satan recognizes this, for in 1:11 and 2:5 Satan says, *"put forth* **your** *hand now and touch."*

Listen to what John MacArthur says about Job in *Our Sufficiency in Christ* :

> Job's story demolishes the notion that we can avoid Satan's attacks if we're sufficiently strong, or skilled enough, or trained in how to wage war against Satan. No one was more spiritually fit than Job. Yet God allowed Satan to ravage him anyway—and there was nothing Job could do about it. Job finally prevailed in the face of Satan's merciless assault, not because he found some secret way to beat the devil, not because he rebuked him or ordered him to desist, but because God was in control all along. He knew how much Job could bear (1 Corinthians 10:13). When Satan reached that limit, God stopped him and his attacks ended. (MacArthur, Crossway Books, 1998, Wheaton, IL, p. 228.)

Make no mistake, Satan is clearly against the people of God. However, he still has to report to the Lord. He can only do what God allows him to do.

Look at Luke 22:31 in its context and write what you see there about Satan's activity with Peter.

_____

_____

_____

In Luke 22:31 Jesus tells Peter that Satan has *"demanded* **permission**" (emphasis mine) to sift him like wheat. Notice first of all that Jesus knew about the coming attack before it happened. He does not prevent it, but He does tell Peter the purpose of it. He says this trial is to sift him like wheat. Grain is sifted to remove the "chaff" or undesirable parts. Jesus knows the outcome as well. He says **"when**, *once you have turned again"* not "if." The implication of this passage is that Satan is under the authority and sovereignty of God.

Because Satan is under the authority and sovereignty of God, the Lord sometimes uses him to accomplish His own purposes. In the cases of Job and Peter, these purposes were for their good, but God's use of Satan is sometimes a mode of punishment. A popular term today in spiritual warfare is "deliverance." But God's working is not always delivering people *from* Satan. Sometimes He delivers them *to* Satan.

Did You Know?
WHEAT

In Jesus' day, wheat was processed in several steps. After harvesting, the next step was threshing. A threshing floor was usually a large circular area of flat rock. The wheat would be spread across the hard ground and oxen or donkeys would tread in a circle, stepping on the grain. Often the animal would pull a "threshing sledge"—a flat, wooden sled upon which a person could stand to provide extra weight. This step would break the grain loose from the stalk and crack open the inedible husk (called "chaff") that surrounded the kernel of wheat. Next the grain would be winnowed by tossing it into the air, allowing the breeze to blow away the chaff as the grain would fall back to the ground.

📖 Look at what Paul writes in 1 Timothy 1:18–20, and write what you learn of God's intended role for Satan in the lives of Hymenaeus and Alexander.

_____

_____

_____

It certainly appears that these men Paul mentions were believers. He speaks of them having *"shipwreck in regard to their faith."* That means they must have a faith. In this case God is using Satan as His tool of chastisement for wandering believers. In 2 Timothy 2:17–18 we are told that Hymenaeus was upsetting the faith of some, *"saying that the resurrection has already taken place."* God uses Satan to bring consequences for this false teaching.

📖 Examine 1 Corinthians 5:1–5 and record what you see there about this concept of delivering someone over to Satan.

_____

_____

_____

So what does it mean for someone to be "delivered over to Satan?" Scripture really doesn't say. It appears that this refers to someone who has not been *"keeping faith and a good conscience"* (1 Timothy 1:19). In other words, the person Paul speaks of is an unrepentant believer. If a believer continues in sin and refuses to repent, apparently sometimes God tells the devil to let him have it, to give him a taste of hell on earth. Paul makes it clear that his salvation is not in question, but God is not willing to let one of His children get comfortable with sin. Sometimes he uses the devil as his agent to judge sin.

SATAN'S MISTAKES

J. Oswald Sanders, in his classic book *Spiritual Leadership*, has one particularly insightful chapter entitled "The Peculiar Perils of Leadership." In pursuing this theme he uses Satan as an example. Until reading his thoughts, I had never really mused on Satan from the vantage point of his being a leader, but he was. He was an archangel—chief among angels. In 1 Timothy 3:6 Paul teaches that the essence of Satan's sin is conceit or pride. Because of this, he is trying to set up a counterfeit kingdom (Revelation 2:13; Ephesians 2:2), but his doom is already sealed. He will not succeed; pride is his undoing. In addressing the issue of pride and its affect on leaders, Sanders says:

> Nothing is more distasteful to God than self-conceit. This first and fundamental sin in essence aims at enthroning self at the expense of God. This was the sin that changed the anointed cherub, guardian of the throne of God, into the foul fiend of hell, and caused his expulsion from heaven…. Of the myriad forms which this sin assumes, none is more abhorrent than spiritual pride. To be proud of spiritual gifts which God has bestowed, or of the position to which His love and grace have elevated us, is to forget that grace is a gift, and that all we have has been

received. Pride is a sin of whose presence its victim is least conscious.... If we are honest, when we measure ourselves by the life of our Lord who humbled Himself even to death on a cross, we cannot but be overwhelmed with the tawdriness and shabbiness, and even the vileness, of our hearts. (Sanders, © 1967, 1975. Moody Bible Institute of Chicago, Moody Press. Pp. 142–3.)

As we will see in today's study, Satan's position of power, instead of satisfying his ambitions, inflamed them and prompted him to covet the position of God Himself.

📖 Look at Ezekiel 28:12–19 and write down everything it reveals about Satan.

_____

_____

_____

_____

An important part of Satan's identity is that he is an angel. Ezekiel 28:13–14 points out that Satan was created and is a "cherub," one form of angel. The cherubim are an order of angels concerned with guarding the holiness of God. Because Satan is an angel, he has the same limitations as angels. That means he is not omnipotent (all-powerful), he is not omniscient (all-knowing), and he is not omnipresent (all places at once). We must guard ourselves from the erroneous notion that Satan is the complimentary opposite of God in this war between good and evil. God has no equals. Satan is a created being. He is an angel with all the limitations of any other angel, and he is accountable to his Creator. If the devil is the opposite of anyone, it would be of the archangel Michael, but he is no match for the Almighty. We see here in Ezekiel that he is an angel in rebellion. Verse 17 indicates that the source of Satan's rebellion is pride in his beauty and wisdom. We see in verses 18–19 that he is destined for fire (Revelation 20:10 indicates it is the lake of fire), and will be no more.

📖 What does Isaiah 14:12–19 reveal of the roots of Satan's fall?

_____

_____

_____

_____

Another aspect of Satan's identity is that he is an angel in rebellion. Isaiah 14:12–19 shows us that he has fallen from heaven because he seeks to be a counterfeit god, to take the rightful place of the one true God. The idea of a fall from heaven is explicitly applied to Satan by Christ in Luke 10:18, making it clear this passage finds its ultimate fulfillment in him. The five *"I will"* statements in Isaiah reveal the self-will of Satan.

In Romans 12:3 the believer is exhorted *"not to think more highly of himself than he ought to think; but to think so as to have sound judgment."* When pride takes root, we cease to think of ourselves accurately. This inflated view of self was Satan's biggest mistake.

"Pride is a sin of whose presence its victim is least conscious"

Oswald Sanders

SATAN'S MOTIVES

The "I will's" of Satan
- *I will ascend to heaven*
- *I will raise my throne*
- *I will sit on the mount*
- *I will ascend above the heights*
- *I will make myself like the Most High*

You know, we normally wouldn't blame a guy for aiming high, but it is a pretty radical ambition to displace God. One of Satan's driving motives is to sit in the seat of God. As we saw yesterday, in Isaiah 14:12–20 he says,

> *I will ascend to heaven, I will raise my throne above the stars of God [this probably refers to the angels], And I will sit on the mount of the assembly in the far north [this points to ruling over either the assembly of the angels or over Israel in the millennium], I will ascend above the heights of the clouds [usurp the glory of God], I will make myself like the Most High [counterfeit God and His work].*

Satan is not creative; he does nothing original. Everything he does is an attempt to imitate God. Notice the central figure. "I." Five times Satan says, "I will." His rebellion (along with every rebellion since) has at its core the desire to be his own god and to answer to no higher authority.

Take a moment to read the passages below and reflect on the fact that to replace God is not Satan's only mistaken ambition. He also desires to incite others to join him in his rebellion.

📖 Genesis 3:1–6

📖 Matthew 4:1–11

📖 1 John 5:19

From the very beginning he has tried to lead believers astray. We see him in the garden as he tempts Adam and Eve to disobey God (Genesis 3:1–6). At the beginning of Christ's earthly ministry Satan targets Him (Matthew 4:1–11). He already has unbelievers on his side, though they don't realize it. 1 John 5:19 says, *"The whole world lies in the power of the evil one."* And he targets believers as well. Peter calls him *"your adversary"* and describes him as prowling about *"like a roaring lion, seeking someone to devour"* (1 Peter 5:8). And if he can't devour you, he'll try to distract you from walking with God.

📖 What does 2 Corinthians 11:3 reveal of Satan's design against believers?

_____

_____

_____

Satan wants us to step outside of God's plan just as he has. He would love to tempt us into direct rebellion with God's commands. If Satan cannot get us into overt sin, however, that doesn't mean we are safe. He still will have succeeded if he can lure us away from simple, pure devotion to Christ. He may even use an imbalanced interest in spiritual warfare to get your eyes on Satan and demons instead of fixed on Jesus where they ought to be.

Don't kid yourself. Satan is no one's friend. Jesus alluded to him as being a thief who aims only to *"steal, kill, and destroy"* (John 10:10). Is it that he genuinely thinks he can outwit God? Or does he understand he cannot defeat God, but simply wants to do as much damage as he can? In either case, we are better armed if we understand his motives up front.

FOR ME TO FOLLOW GOD

Between graduating from college and going into the ministry, I spent several years in the restaurant business. At the end of a long shift I could often be found counting up the day's receipts. I became adept at quickly and accurately counting large stacks of bills. Because paper money was so often in my hands, I was well–equipped to recognize something was amiss one night with a particular twenty-dollar bill. It didn't feel right. Upon closer scrutiny, I realized it didn't look quite right either. Through a brief investigation I confirmed that one of our cashiers had accepted a counterfeit bill. In my managerial training, I had been given a brief crash course in the danger of counterfeits, but it would not have been wise to spend too much time on all the different types of fake money that could come our way. We were warned, but the real key was not in becoming an expert on counterfeits, but in being familiar with the real thing. There is a tangible parallel to this in spiritual warfare.

I would not go so far as to say that understanding Satan is the most important aspect of spiritual warfare. We do need to know we have an enemy, and we should not be ignorant of his schemes. However, we must not forget that he wears many disguises. The greatest defense against deception is to be well-versed in truth.

APPLY As you consider your own view of Satan and the demonic realm, where would you place yourself on the continuum below?

I————————————————————————————I
Think too little of   Balanced view   Unhealthy interest
Satan and demons   in dark things

When you consider our culture today and the fallen world in which we live, what are some ways you see that Satan exerts his influence by appearing as an "angel of light"?

_____

_____

_____

What do you need to do to combat this influence in your own arena?

_____

_____

_____

Certainly one way we can counter the deception of Satan's tricks is simply to remind ourselves that he aims to represent himself as something positive and good. We must be alert to the possibility of being deceived. Only when we have armed ourselves with truth are we in a position to combat his lies. This Bible study is one proactive thing you are doing to guard yourself.

APPLY Take a moment to glance through this week's lesson. Are there any other specific action points that you sense the Lord is prompting you toward?

_____

_____

_____

_____

_____

Why not close out this lesson by committing those action points to the Lord in a written prayer, also dedicating this entire study process to Him.

_____

_____

_____

_____

_____

_____

_____

_____

_____

_____

_____

_____

Works Cited

1. C. S. Lewis, *The Screwtape Letters* (New York: Macmillan, 1961), 3.

We must be alert to the possibility of being deceived.

Notes

2

Satan's Methods

ountless books have been written about the successful strategies of General Robert E. Lee in the American Civil War. Even though the Union armies were the eventual winners, Lee handed the Yankees a string of defeats against overwhelming odds. His troops were vastly outnumbered and extremely ill-equipped. Although Lee's troops were in a poor position to attack or defend, the Union spent four years and incurred five times as many casualties to defeat the Rebel forces. In fact, the war was past the halfway point before the Yankees were able to claim a victory, which occurred against General Lee on the fields at Gettysburg. At the bloody battle of Antietam, it is estimated that Lee's Army of Northern Virginia was outnumbered by as many as three to one. With more than 23,000 casualties, September 17, 1862, is the bloodiest single-day battle in American history, with more than twice as many casualties as the D-Day invasion in World War II. Although the South had fewer casualties than the North, they could ill afford them. The Union Army of the Potomac had kept ample troops in reserve, while the South utilized every man in battle. The Civil War would have ended in little more than a year if General McClellan had successfully pressed his advantage there. However, Lee was somehow able to outmaneuver McClellan's Army of the Potomac and return his troops safely to Virginia.

Prior to the Civil War, General Lee had fought in the war with Mexico but had never commanded troops in battle. His only

With over 23,000 casualties, September 17th more than doubly outranks the D-Day invasion in World War II as the bloodiest single-day battle in American history.

experience at leading soldiers into conflict occurred at the U.S. Military Arsenal at Harper's Ferry when John Brown and his handful of followers briefly captured the facility and hoped to supply slaves with weapons for revolt. However, when he took command of the Confederate troops, Lee performed like a seasoned veteran from the very beginning. The Seven Days' Battles, the Second Battle of Bull Run, the Battle of Fredericksburg, and the Battle of Chancellorsville are considered his greatest victories.

How was Lee able to repeatedly defeat his opponents despite insufficient troops and inadequate supplies? He was a brilliant general, to be sure. And a fundamental aspect of his genius was his knowledge of the enemy. He knew what opposing generals would do, almost before they had even decided. Lee had studied with most of the Union Generals at West Point and knew them personally. He knew how they thought and how they fought. On September 18, 1872, the day after the battle at Antietam, Lee predicted accurately that McClellan would play it conservatively and not launch a major assault until the following day. By renewing skirmishes throughout that day, he convinced McClellan that he still had enough troops to continue the battle. That night, under the cover of darkness, Lee ordered his battered troops back to safety across the Potomac. One of the keys to his string of successes was that he had mastered the schemes and strategies of his enemy. Similarly, one of the keys for us in spiritual battle is to know the schemes and strategies of our enemy.

SATAN DECEIVES

How do you picture Satan? Is he a wiry little figure in a red suit with a pitchfork and pointed tail? Or perhaps you imagine him as far more diabolical. Maybe you see him in such movie characters as Freddy from the *Nightmare on Elm Street* movies, or Jason from the *Friday the 13th* series. The truth is, Satan's most effective methods are completely unlike those images. Rather than appearing as overtly evil, he comes as an angel of light. Then again, I suppose that he likes to deceive us even in our idea of his deceptions. His trickery isn't limited to clouding our view of him. He also tries to deceive believers in their view of God and what He says. The best illustration of this happened in the very beginning of human history. Satan's rebellion first stains humanity in the Garden of Eden.

In Genesis 3:1–6 we see Eve engaging in a conversation with the serpent. Why, from what the text says about what he is like and what he does, is this a bad idea?

_____

_____

_____

The text reveals two negative qualities of Satan: what he is like—*"...more crafty than any beast of the field"*, and what he does—he calls into question the revealed will of God. He asks, *"Indeed, has God said...?"* He also exaggerates the limitations that God's will imposes on mankind. He misquotes God when he asks, *"You shall not eat from **any** tree of the garden?"*

Compare Genesis 3:1–6 with 2 Corinthians 11:3 and 12–15, and with 1 Timothy 2:14 and write what you learn about Satan's activities.

📖 2 Corinthians 11:3

_____

_____

_____

📖 2 Corinthians 11:12–15

_____

_____

_____

_____

📖 1 Timothy 2:14

_____

_____

_____

_____

Word Study
ANGEL

Satan appears as an angel of light. The word "angel" (Gr. *aggelos*) literally means "messenger." This meaning underscores the reality that much of Satan's deception centers in incorrect messages—lies.

We see in 2 Corinthians 11:3 that the serpent *"deceived Eve by his craftiness."* Paul says in 1 Timothy 2:14 that she was *"being deceived."* Satan and his workers operate through deception and disguise. In fact, we are told in 2 Corinthians 11:14 that he *"disguises himself as an angel of light."*

When dealing with an enemy who doesn't practice truth, one must be especially careful to not take anything at face value. Eve should have allowed God's words to be her authority, but as soon as Satan tricked her into calling what God had said into question, it was only a matter of time before she went her own independent way. When we make ourselves the judge of the validity of God's words, transgression is inevitable.

SATAN CASTS DOUBT

Satan's Methods

DAY TWO

R ecently, while visiting some relatives in another town, I volunteered to help them on a repair project, and I made a trip to the hardware store for supplies. Although I followed the directions, I began to doubt that I was going the right way, and eventually I convinced myself I was on the wrong track. I finally gave up and returned empty-handed, only to discover that I had turned around less than two blocks from my destination. Doubt is a powerful tool, especially in the hands of an enemy.

📖 Look at Genesis 3:4–5. How does Satan cast doubt on the things God had said concerning the forbidden tree?

_____

_____

_____

_____

Eve could have sent Satan running simply by taking God at His word and not buying into Satan's lies.

Let's see what we can learn about Satan's methods from this story. Satan's first objective is to twist what God has said and to place Him in a negative light. Notice how Satan misquotes God: *"Indeed, has God said 'You shall not eat from any tree of the garden'?"* Satan knew that was not what God had said, but he was trying to get Eve to focus on God's boundaries instead of His freedoms. Look at what comes next. When Eve corrects Satan's statement, he quickly begins to sow doubt about God's honesty and motives. He says, *"You surely shall not die! For God knows that in the day you eat from it your eyes will be opened, and you will be like God, knowing good and evil."* He is suggesting that God has not told the truth, and he is implying that God is withholding something good from Adam and Eve. Nothing could be further from the truth. Eve could simply have sent Satan running by taking God at His word and not buying into Satan's lies. Instead of keeping her eyes on God, she put them on the promises of the deceiver.

📖 Look at John 10:10. What does Jesus say here is the objective of one who would steal the sheep?

_____

_____

_____

In John 10:10 Jesus indicates that *"the thief comes only to steal, and kill, and destroy."* He is referring specifically to false teachers and false messiahs whose objective was to draw people away from the Lord, and obviously Satan was chief among them. If he can't establish his own kingdom, then he wants to do everything he can to destroy God's kingdom.

📖 What do you learn of Satan in John 8:44 and 1 John 3:8?

_____

_____

_____

In John 8:44 Jesus teaches that Satan is a murderer and a liar. First John 3:8 shows us he has sinned from the very beginning. Everything he does is negative because his aim is destruction.

Satan isn't very original in his attacks. When he finds something that works, he sticks with it. He still uses those same strategies on believers today. He, and those who are allied with him, continue to twist what God has said; they persist in getting us to focus on God's boundaries instead of His freedoms. They also try to cause us to doubt that God's words are true, and they attempt to make us believe that God is withholding something good from us with His restrictions. But everything God gives is good, and every restriction He sets is for our benefit. And everything He says is true. The essence of faith, therefore, is to simply take God at His word. We believe that what He says is more reliable than how we feel. We believe that what He says He will do, He really will do, and we live accordingly.

SATAN AMBUSHES

Don't you wish you could plan your battles? Wouldn't it be great if you always knew in advance when and where the confrontation would occur? A person is most vulnerable when the attack is least expected, and it is helpful to remind ourselves of this. We need to realize that the devil looks for times of weakness to attack—when we are tired or unguarded. An illustration of this method is seen in his efforts to tempt Jesus in the wilderness.

📖 Look at Matthew 4:1–11 and write what you observe of the timing of his attack and the human needs and desires he seems to aim at.

_____

_____

_____

_____

We looked at this encounter briefly in lesson 1, but there is more to be learned from the method of his attack on Jesus. First, notice when Satan begins his attack—it was after Jesus had fasted forty days and forty nights. There is no chivalry with Satan; he is not going to fight fairly. He always tries to catch us when we are weakest. Secondly, he attacks Jesus' reputation. Notice he says, "**If** *You are the Son of God. . . .*" Jesus knew He was the Son of God, but Satan wants Him to feel He has to prove something. Notice also that Satan hits Jesus where He is weak: His hunger. Satan says, "*Command that these stones become bread.*" Of course, Jesus' response is significant too. He doesn't try to argue with Satan; He just quotes Scripture. Jesus said, "*It is written, 'Man shall not live on bread alone, but on every word that proceeds out of the mouth of God.*'" Satan has tried appealing to "*the lust of the flesh*" (1 John 2:16), but that doesn't work, so he moves on to "*the boastful pride of life.*" He tries to tempt Jesus to prove He is the Son of God.

We must recognize that the Bible can be misapplied and misused, especially when we come to it with our own agenda. Our beliefs must not be based on a verse here or there, but on the whole counsel of God. In his quote from Psalm 91:11–12 Satan omits a sentence that does not suit his purposes, violating one of the fundamental rules of Bible study: "every perceived truth must be consistent with the context it comes from." We always get into trouble if we try to understand and apply a verse of Scripture without taking the time to read it in its context.

I once attended a lecture on the subject of personal discipline and leading a disciplined life. One of the verses quoted was Hebrews 12:11 which reads, "*All discipline for the moment seems not to be joyful, but sorrowful; yet to those who have been trained by it, afterwards it yields the peaceful fruit of righteousness.*" The point the speaker was making was that it isn't fun to apply discipline to your personal life, but if you do, you will be better for it. The point was true, but this was the wrong verse to support it. If you read the context of Hebrews 12:11, you discover that the "discipline" spoken of here is not the personal discipline we use when we try to order our lives and stick to a schedule or cultivate a habit. The context is speaking of when the Lord chastens His children. When I later brought this to the speaker's attention

Our beliefs must not be based on a verse here or there, but on the whole counsel of God.

Everything Satan offers Jesus is within God's will—but it isn't in God's way.

in private, I learned that they had come up with the idea for the talk, and then begun to search for verses to support the idea. This is an easy way to distort the Bible. We should never go to the Bible looking for support for a conclusion we have already reached. We must let the Bible speak for itself, and then draw our conclusions based on the principles of the whole counsel of God in His word.

Let's get back to Jesus' temptation. Satan has tried to tempt Jesus with the lust of the flesh and the boastful pride of life, but neither worked. So now Satan throws his last pitch: *"the lust of the eyes."* He offers Jesus all the kingdoms of the world, and their glory; he said to Him, *"All these things I will give You, if You fall down and worship me."* Then Jesus said to him, *"Go, Satan! For it is written, 'You shall worship the Lord your God, and serve Him only.'"* Then the devil left Him; and behold, angels came and began to minister to Him."

Now let me ask you something. Is there something magical in Jesus saying, *"Go, Satan"*? I don't think so. For if that were all it took, why didn't Jesus avoid the whole battle and do that first? Here is a key observation: Jesus knew there was a purpose in the battle. He didn't seek it out. He didn't look for the devil, but He didn't run either. He just held His ground and kept His eyes on the Father.

One important thing to recognize about Satan's temptation of Jesus is that everything he offered Jesus is within the will of God. It was God's will that Jesus be fed; it was God's will that Jesus be protected; it was God's will that Jesus rule and reign over all the kingdoms of the earth. So everything Satan offered Him was within God's will—it just wasn't God's way. Satan offered shortcuts, or ways for Jesus to provide for Himself instead of being satisfied with God's provision and timing based on His infinite and perfect wisdom.

SATAN DISGUISES HIMSELF

In the animal and plant kingdoms, disguise is one of the most common and effective tools for survival. For example, the Sepiola squid produces a cloud of ink in the color and shape of a squid when it is threatened by a predator. It then changes color and escapes while the attacker pursues a mirage. Numerous frogs and lizards are camouflaged to look like their surroundings. However, not all deception in the animal world is defensive. Some use camouflage and disguise to trap their prey. The Malaysian preying mantis looks like a flower and lures unsuspecting bees into its grasp. The female Photuris firefly mimics the blinking signal of another species of firefly and lures their males close enough to be eaten. Even flowers practice this game of deception. Some orchids deceive male insects by resembling their female partners in order to facilitate their pollination.

Satan, like these plants and animals, uses deception to accomplish his purposes. In 2 Corinthians Paul confronts a church that had been infiltrated by false teachers, men who for the sake of personal gain were corrupting and distorting the Word of God.

APPLY What do you learn from Paul in 2 Corinthians 11:13–15 about one of Satan's most effective methods?

_____

_____

_____

Satan is far more effective at deceiving when he disguises himself. He doesn't want us to recognize him as an obvious enemy. He would much rather hide under a guise of light and goodness. That is why he loves to work through religion. Why else would there be so many different ones? In reality, not everyone who claims to be a follower of God really is.

So, how do we protect ourselves? How do we know if a teacher is of God or is just a wolf in sheep's clothing? By making the Bible our standard instead of people or experiences. Every message we hear and every experience we have must be interpreted in light of what the Word of God says. And by this, I do not mean simply that we find a Bible verse to support what we believe. I mean that we must learn to handle the Bible correctly, and we must let it and only it shape our convictions. That is our security.

📖 In John 8:44, Jesus rebukes the Pharisees and unbelieving Jews. Look at what He says there and write what you learn about the devil.

_____

_____

_____

_____

It is not that every single thing Satan says is a lie, because sometimes he weaves truth into what he says to lure us in. But his end goal is deception and not truth. Even when he communicates truth, it is twisted to fit his purposes, and the result is untruth.

One of Satan's most powerful methods is cloaking himself in religion. It is worthwhile to remind ourselves that it was not the pagans and heathen who crucified Jesus and persecuted and martyred the apostles. It was the religious crowd who distorted the Word of God to fit their own desires and who didn't walk in relationship with God.

FOR ME TO FOLLOW GOD

In Ephesians 6:11 we are told that when we put on the armor of God we are *"able to stand firm against the schemes of the devil."* The Greek word for "schemes" there is *methodeia*. Sound familiar? It is where we get our English word "methods." It means "the following or pursuit of an orderly procedure." Our enemy, Satan, is actually quite predictable when you understand his methods. That is why such a study is so practical and helpful in spiritual warfare. If we are to successfully follow God in the hostile environment of a fallen world, we must know our enemy and how he attacks.

> *"Satan ... has a thousand stratagems at his command for deceiving. So much the more ought believers to be supplied with spiritual arms for fighting, and so much the more earnestly ought they to keep watch with vigilance and sobriety."* [1]
>
> **John Calvin**

Satan's Methods

DAY FIVE

"For all that is in the world, the lust of the flesh and the lust of the eyes and the boastful pride of life, is not from the Father, but is from the world."

1 John 2:16

Was the fact that Satan is a deceiver a new truth for you? Probably not. Most likely you have heard that many times before. Yet it is a truth easily forgotten. If we believe we live on a playground rather than a battlefield, we will not exercise the caution that we should.

In which of these areas of temptation do you tend to recognize Satan's deception easily?

___ Lust of the Flesh (Pleasure)
___ Lust of the Eyes (Materialism)
___ Boastful Pride of Life (Pride)

In which areas are you prone to be duped by the enemy?

___ Lust of the Flesh (Pleasure)
___ Lust of the Eyes (Materialism)
___ Boastful Pride of Life (Pride)

As we saw in the case of Eve in the garden, one of the strategies of the devil is to tempt us to doubt the truthfulness of what God says and the goodness of His motives toward us.

APPLY What are some situations where you are tempted to doubt what God says is true?

_____

_____

_____

_____

What are some situations where you are tempted to doubt that God's will for you is good?

_____

_____

_____

_____

_____

What do you need to do in order to guard against this strategy of the devil?

_____

_____

_____

_____

_____

As we look to the Scriptures, we can find patterns to Satan's attack. As we saw in Matthew 4, he came to Jesus at a point of physical weakness (after forty days of fasting). In David's sin with Bathsheba, the temptation came at a point of idleness. Elijah was tempted with fear and suicidal thoughts after a period of great spiritual victory on Mt. Carmel. Moses was tempted to strike the rock in the context of the grumbling and complaints of those whom he led. The book of James teaches that we are vulnerable to temptation during periods of trial and testing. Consider the list below and circle the ones that have led to stumbling in your own life.

Times of physical weakness
Periods of idleness
After great spiritual victory
When those around you grumble and complain
During seasons of trials
Other _____

What lessons can you learn from past experiences that will help you in the future?

_____

_____

_____

_____

_____

_____

Remember, the key to spiritual victory is not us overcoming sin and the devil. It is Jesus overcoming us. Why not close out this week by writing a prayer to the Lord, expressing your surrender to Him in the areas of vulnerability in your life?

_____

_____

_____

_____

_____

_____

_____

_____

_____

_____

_____

_____

_____

Works Cited

1. John Calvin, commentary on John 8:44, *Calvin's Commentaries, Vol. 34: John, Part I*, tr. by John King, [1847-50], at sacred-texts.com, Calvin Translation Society.

Notes

3

Dealing with Demons

The 1973 film *The Exorcist* brought the concept of demon-possession to the forefront of Western thought. Based on the 1971 book by William Peter Blatty, the plot revolved around the demonic possession of a young girl. Her mother sought the assistance of two priests as they fought to rid her of the tormenting demon. Many of our impressions of demons and demon possession have been shaped more by that movie than by what the Scriptures teach. That the film grossed over $400 million worldwide testifies to the impact this dramatization had on shaping the modern concept of demonic possession.[1] Although fictional, the book was inspired by a documented exorcism allegedly performed in 1949 on a thirteen-year-old boy. Blatty heard of the event while a student at the Jesuit and Catholic school, Georgetown University. He used the diary of one of the priests who performed the exorcism as the basis of his book.[2] The diary records details duplicated in the book and movie such as the shaking bed, scratches and words appearing on the child, a vial of holy water being thrown across the room, and a bookcase moving on its own. This personal record does not give any account of a 360 degree head-turn, impaling on a bloody crucifix, or pea green projectile vomiting.

Was the boy actually possessed by a demon? Experts disagree on this. A 1993 book entitled *Possessed: The True Story of an Exorcism* by Thomas B. Allen thoroughly researched the original account and claims that it is true. Apparently, the boy's favorite aunt, a spiritualist from St. Louis, introduced the child

How we view demons and demon possession has been shaped more by the movie The Exorcist than by what the Scriptures teach.

to the Ouija board. Allen suggests that the boy may have channeled his own possession by playing the board game.[3] That the boy's parents sought help from priests is clear. The eyewitness accounts tell a dramatic story punctuated with apparently supernatural circumstances. The priest who took the lead in the procedure fasted for the entire 40 days of the exorcism. The process concluded on April 18, 1949, the day after Easter. As frightening as the movie was, it is even more disturbing to reflect on the actual events that inspired it.

How should one handle such a dark and terrifying account? I take you back to the previously quoted advice of C. S. Lewis on the two dangers to avoid regarding the devil and demons: "One is to disbelieve...the other is to believe, and to feel an excessive and unhealthy interest." Satan is pleased by either response. Instead, we should interpret this and any seemingly demonic experience by what God's Word has to say. I am convinced that Satan is willing to induce almost any experience or illusion that will create confusion and fear. We know God's Word is true—the same cannot be said about experiences, *especially* when it comes to the demonic realm! So instead of dwelling on a possible Satanic experience or a Hollywood dramatization, I suggest we go to the Bible for understanding.

WHAT DEMONS ARE

There are different theories as to the origin of demons. A heathen Greek view was that they were the souls of evil persons who had died. Others have suggested that they are the disembodied spirits of a race of people created before Adam. Neither of these ideas has any support in Scripture. Genesis 6:1–4 states,

> *Now it came about, when men began to multiply on the face of the land, and daughters were born to them, that the sons of God saw that the daughters of men were beautiful; and they took wives for themselves, whomever they chose. Then the LORD said, "My Spirit shall not strive with man forever, because he also is flesh; nevertheless his days shall be one hundred and twenty years." The Nephilim were on the earth in those days, and also afterward, when the sons of God came in to the daughters of men, and they bore children to them. Those were the mighty men who were of old, men of renown.*

Some have conjectured that these verses refer to angels cohabiting with human women and that their offspring are demons. The problem with this idea is that angels are called *"ministering spirits"* (Hebrews 1:14). A spirit, not having a physical body, cannot cohabit with a person. God did not create us that way. The traditional view—and the one that seems to make the most sense based on what Scripture reveals—is that demons are fallen angels who joined Satan in his rebellion against God.

📖 What do you learn in Matthew 12:24 and 25:41 about Satan's relationship with demons?

_____

_____

_____

Dealing with Demons

DAY ONE

📖 *Doctrine*
ANGELS AND HUMANS?

Reasons to conclude Gen. 6 is not talking about angels cohabiting with humans:

• Angels are spirits; they don't have physical bodies.

• Angels are not male or female.

• If cohabitation were possible, why would such offspring be giants?

• Why would angels want to settle down and live on earth?

• The emphasis of the context is on the sin of man, not the fall of angels.

• God's judgment was because of what humans did, not actions of angels (see v.3).

• Nephilim are also present after Noah's flood, which would require a second period of cohabitation.

• The most likely interpretation is that the "sons of God" refers to the godly line of Seth intermarrying with women from the ungodly line of Cain.

While considering Satan, we noted that he is an angel, and in Matthew 12:24 he is called *"the ruler of the demons."* Whatever demons are, they are under Satan's leadership. This implies that they are like him. By inference we can surmise that demons are most likely angels who have joined Satan in his rebellion. And in fact, Matthew 25:41, in speaking of the eternal fires of hell, says that they are reserved for *"the devil and his angels."* Demons are his partners and will meet the same end as he.

📖 Look up Revelation 12:4 and record what you learn there about Satan and demons.

_____

_____

_____

In Revelation 12:4 we see that the dragon *"swept away a third of the stars of heaven and threw them to the earth."* Verse 9 of this chapter identifies the dragon plainly, saying he is *"the serpent of old who is called the devil and Satan."* Most scholars interpret the *"stars of heaven"* as referencing angels and take this to mean that when Satan fell, he took a third of the angels with him. The good news is that this means they are outnumbered two-to-one.

📖 Reflect on 2 Peter 2:4 and Jude 1:6. What else do you learn about the number of demons active on the planet?

_____

_____

_____

In 2 Peter 2:4 we learn that some angels who sinned have already been cast into hell, and are being held in *"pits of darkness"* awaiting judgment. Jude 1:6, probably talking about the same group, indicates these fallen angels are kept in chains. The reason for this punishment is that they didn't stay where they were supposed to stay, but *"abandoned their proper abode."* So apparently, Satan's army has been reduced from its original size. If in fact they originally numbered one-third of all angels, the percentage active in spiritual war is now less.

Scripture never tells us clearly how many angels there are. The most definitive expression in the Bible numbers them at *"myriads of myriads, and thousands of thousands"* (Revelation 5:11). This indicates a rather large number since *myriad*—the Greek term for ten thousand—was the largest number that language expressed. If the passage meant ten thousand times ten thousand, that would indicate there are one billion angels. Since both times the word is plural, a literal number would be many times more than that. More likely, this phrase should simply be understood to say they are beyond numbering. If demons represent one third, the bottom line is still that Satan's army is far outnumbered by God's. Even if the ratio moved in the opposite direction, all the angels ever created are no match for the all-powerful Creator!

Did You Know?
MYRIADS

Since the Greek word translated "myriads" was the largest number in that culture, it was taken to mean "innumerable." In the Septuagint (the Greek translation of the Old Testament) this same word is used in Genesis 24:60 in the blessing given to Rebekah, wife of Isaac, through whom Abraham's promise would be realized: "'May you, our sister, Become thousands of ten thousands, And may your descendants possess the gate of those who hate them'" (emphasis added).

WHAT DEMONS KNOW

Can a demon read your mind? Is a demon able to know what you will do before you do it? Does such a being have the ability to see its own future? What does a demon understand about God and His world? What does it know of Bible prophecy and its own ordained future? These are questions of consequence with practical application. Opinions abound and diverge in many conflicting directions. Rather than us drawing conclusions from our opinions or limited subjective experience, let us look to the Bible to answer such questions. Understanding the truth about demons helps us to view them properly and without fear.

📖 Read Mark 1:23–24 and write a brief summary of what you learn there about what demons understand.

_____

_____

_____

_____

When Jesus visits the synagogue at Capernaum, He encounters a demon-possessed man. It is amazing enough that He would have to deal with demon possession with someone attending the synagogue. What this passage reveals about demons is equally amazing. We learn from Mark 1:23–24 that demons know who Jesus is—His person. They recognize Him as the "Holy One of God" (i.e. "the Messiah")—His position. Third, they recognize Him as One who is able to destroy them—His power.

📖 From Matthew 8:28–32, identify what knowledge we can glean about demons from this encounter.

_____

_____

_____

_____

As Jesus enters the region of the Gadarenes on the east shore of the Sea of Galilee, He meets up with two men who are demon possessed. These demons, speaking through those they possess, immediately recognize Jesus as the *"Son of God."* The unique dimension this discussion reveals is that the demons acknowledge an appointed time in the future for their judgment. They know to whom they will answer, how they will answer, and when.

📖 What do you learn from James 2:19 regarding demons and what they believe?

_____

_____

_____

James 2:19 makes it clear that demons believe there is one God. They are true monotheists. What is more, that thought makes them shudder. Their

"You believe that God is one. You do well; the demons also believe, and shudder."

James 2:19

belief is not mere intellectual assent or theoretical abstraction; they truly dread meeting their maker, and they know what awaits them.

Perhaps the most important point these verses reveal is that demons know they are no match for the Lord. They know His power and that they are answerable to Him. Satan and his minions would like us to think more highly of them than we should, but they all know who is greatest.

WHAT DEMONS ARE ABLE TO DO

Although yesterday's study focused specifically on what demons know, we also saw some examples of what demons are able to do. We learned from the encounter in the Gadarenes that they can make those whom they possess extremely violent. The two demon-possessed men were so violent that people had to avoid the area. We also learned from that incident that they can possess animals and cause them harm. It seems clear that demons can influence our world and its inhabitants. How far can their influence go? Today we'll investigate additional demonic encounters in Scripture to discover more of what demons are able to do.

Look at Matthew 9:32–33 and write what you learn there about what demons are able to do.

_____

_____

_____

The encounter in Galilee with a mute, demon-possessed man broadens our understanding of what demons are able to do. It is clear from this narrative that the demon was the cause of the man's inability to speak. As soon as the demon had gone, he was able to talk. It is worth noting that in the next verse, Matthew 9:34, the Pharisees acknowledge Jesus' ability to cast out the demon, even though they are unwilling to credit this as a work of God. Apparently demons are able to exert control over those they possess to a significant degree. Not only can demons speak through people as we saw in previous encounters, but they can also prevent people from speaking.

Examine the demonic incident in Luke 13:10–16 and record your insights on the ability of demons to affect people.

_____

_____

_____

Luke reports yet another demonic event here in chapter 13—a woman with a sickness *"caused by a spirit."* Because of this demon, the woman was bent over and unable to stand upright for eighteen years. This gives us a clear sense that demon-possession is no temporary affliction. Jesus speaks to the woman, lays hands on her, and immediately the demon leaves. As soon as the spirit is gone, her affliction leaves as well. She is able to stand erect for the first time in nearly two decades. No wonder she is glorifying God!

When I reflect on this encounter, I am reminded of the exorcism we mentioned at the beginning of this week—the one that inspired the movie *The Exorcist*. Priests wrestled with the supposed demon for forty days, yet Jesus' victory was immediate. There were no ecclesiastical gyrations. No special formulas were employed. There was no need for multiple attempts. In fact, there appears to have been no wrestling at all. Jesus just spoke the word. This one episode doesn't mean all cases are easy, but it does indicate that casting out a demon doesn't have to be a prolonged process.

Reflect on Mark 5:1–13, a parallel account of the demons cast into the swine. Identify what new information you gather about the circumstances of this encounter and the things demons are able to do.

_____

_____

_____

Did You Know?
LEGION

The name "Legion" with which the demons identified themselves was a cultural term applied in Roman society to the military. The term was derived from the Latin word legio, meaning "military levy or conscription." During the days of the Roman Republic, a typical legion consisted of about 4,200 foot soldiers and 300 cavalry. In the Imperial Rome of Jesus' day, that number grew to 5,200 foot soldiers plus auxiliaries.

Mark's account reveals several possible characteristics demon possession. Apparently demons can exert supernatural strength through a possessed individual. This man was too strong for any man to subdue and was able to break chains and shackles to pieces. Demons can force those whom they possess to harm themselves: *"he was...gashing himself with stones."* Multiple demons are able to inhabit a single person: *"'My name is Legion; for we are many.'"* This is reinforced by the fact that they eventually inhabit a herd of swine numbering over 2,000. Although Matthew's account mentions two individuals, this does not contradict Mark's record. Obviously the man possessed by a legion of demons was the main character in the story, and Mark saw the other man as peripheral, as does Luke's account in Luke 8:26–39.

These fallen angels extend the authority and impact of Satan by doing his bidding. They can inflict diseases, they can possess men or animals, and they try to hinder the work of God by interfering with the spiritual growth of His people. One of the specific ways they do this is by spreading false doctrines. In 1 Timothy 4:1 we learn that in the end times people will be influenced by *"deceitful spirits and doctrines of demons."* It is easy to blame the false teachers for spreading theses doctrines and to think that those who follow them are innocent victims. However, this is not always the case. While some may follow in ignorance, we see in 2 Timothy 4:3–4 that a time will come when people will not endure sound doctrine; *"but wanting to have their ears tickled, they will* **accumulate for themselves** *teachers in accordance to* **their own desires***; and will turn away their ears from the truth, and will turn aside to myths"* (emphasis mine).

What I want you to notice is the part the listeners play in this. Without people whose flesh wants to hear what the false teachers have to say, they would be out of a job very quickly.

We have examined several accounts of demon possession. When we say that demons can possess people, we mean a demon indwelling a person, controlling and influencing him. Usually, but not always, a demon-possessed person seems to be out of his mind. An exception to this is the slave girl with a spirit of divination cast out by Paul during his ministry in Philippi (Acts 16:16–18). It should also be said that demon possession is not the same thing as demonic influence. The key is whether the demon is working from the outside or the inside.

How far can a demon go? We will address that question more fully in later lessons when we begin dealing with the believer's response in spiritual warfare, but for the time being, suffice it to say that a demon can only go as far as God allows. In fact, God sometimes uses demons for His own purposes, as He also does with Satan. We see this illustrated with King Saul, for in 1 Samuel 16:14 we learn that it was an *"evil spirit from the Lord"* that tormented him. In 2 Corinthians 12:7 Paul tells us that his thorn in the flesh was *"a messenger* [lit. angel] *of Satan"* and yet it clearly fulfilled a purpose of God.

DEALING WITH DEMON POSSESSION

I do believe demon-possession is real and not relegated to the days of antiquity. It is not beyond the realm of possibility that we may encounter such a challenging situation, especially as we seek to reach the lost of this world. It seems apparent from the Bible record that God can and does use His servants to cast out demons. How does one cast out a demon? What is the correct process? Let's take a look at four different accounts and see what the Scriptures reveal.

Look at Jesus casting out a demon in Luke 4:33–35 and write what specifics you observe of His process.

_____

_____

_____

_____

In this instance Jesus casts out the demon with a simple command. He rebukes the demon, saying *"Be quiet and come out of him!"* Why did Jesus silence the demon? On another occasion, depicted in Mark 1:34, the text indicates that Jesus did not want demons stating who He was in the early part of His ministry. This method of verbal command seems to be indicative of Jesus' normal practice. In Matthew 8:16 we are told, *"they brought to Him many who were demon-possessed; and He cast out the spirits with a word"* (see also Luke 4:36). In Mark 7 He even casts a demon out of a person who is in another location just by His words. Only in Luke 13, when he healed the woman who was bent double, do we see a case where it appears He incorporated laying hands on her.

Observe Peter casting out demons in Acts 5:15–16 and record the method he employed.

_____

_____

_____

Little is said of the specific methods employed, except that we are told some hoped simply for Peter's shadow to fall upon the afflicted person. This would indicate that Peter's actions did not appear to be complicated or require great exertion.

Did You Know?

DEMON POSSESSION

Although we do see demon-possession mentioned in the Old Testament, there is no Biblical record of a demon being cast out until Jesus comes.

📖 Philip's ministry to Samaria in Acts 8:6–7 included healing those demon-possessed. What, if anything, can you learn there about his process?

_____

_____

_____

_____

Again, little is said about how Phillip performed this ministry, but it is important to note that the passage calls this service *"signs."* In other words, the act of casting out a demon here was not an end in itself, but an attesting miracle to accompany the primary focus of *"preaching the word"* (Acts 8:4) to lead them to Christ.

📖 What can you conclude from what you see in Acts 16:16–18 about Paul's method of casting out demons?

_____

_____

_____

Once again, the only evident action is to command the spirit to leave. As if for emphasis, Luke adds *"it came out at that very moment."* The one thing that is absent from each of these different accounts is a complex system. There were no mystical incantations or spiritual gyrations used. It seems to be a simple issue of making use of the authority of God.

It troubles me to see the complicated schemes that some ministers employ, as if only the very learned and trained in a specific method would dare to confront the demonic. I do not mean to make light of what is a very serious spiritual matter. However, if there were a prescribed system, we would find the steps of such a process modeled in Scripture. God's Word provides us with *"everything pertaining to life and godliness"* (2 Peter 1:3–4). If we needed a special exorcism program, it would be spelled out in the Bible.

Dealing with Demons

DAY FIVE

FOR ME TO FOLLOW GOD

My list of hobbies includes snorkeling and spearfishing. I'm not one of those who would enjoy lying on the beach in the hot sun and doing nothing but baking. If I am at the ocean, I want to be in it. When I first began to snorkel, I briefly thought about sharks, but didn't worry too much. I freaked out a bit when I first saw a shark in open water, but in retrospect, I laugh at my panic. The shark was pretty tiny and paid no attention to me whatsoever. It really was no threat at all. By the time I took up spearfishing, I had a pretty cavalier attitude about entering the shark's habitat. All that changed, however, on an isolated beach in the Bahamas in 1997. I had just entered the water and wasn't very far from shore. I spied an edible fish and tried to position myself to get a shot. Suddenly I caught movement in my peripheral vision. I turned just as an eight foot shark charged me. I jabbed it on the nose with my spear and deterred it briefly, but then it lunged at me again. I didn't have time to think—merely to react—but all the while I was backpedaling toward shore. I delivered a second forceful poke to the shark's nose, and he backed away a bit. I didn't stick around to see if he had another charge in him, and was glad to get out of the water in one piece.

You might think that after such a close call I would never get back in the ocean again, but that isn't the case. I still love to snorkel and spearfish. But I can assure you I was much more teachable on the subject of sharks after that experience. I familiarized myself with the dangers, how to interpret if a shark is hostile or threatened, and what behaviors I should avoid. I've probably seen a hundred since that encounter. Ironically, rather than being scared away, the more I have learned and observed, the less I am unnerved by the sight of a shark. I am much better informed. I treat them with appropriate respect, but I am not afraid of them.

This week we've gone through a different sort of lesson. Understanding demons may seem to be just a theoretical exercise for you. However, scripture teaches that they are real and do inhabit our world. We needn't fear them—the only being the Bible tells us to fear is God. Gaining a Biblical understanding of demons ought to diminish our fears. It certainly should not add to them. Talking about spirits not aligned with God, John stated, *"Greater is He who is in you than he who is in the world"* (1 John 4:4).

On the scale below, place a circle over where you think you were before this lesson in your anxiety about demons. Then place a square on where you perceive yourself to be after this week's lesson. Try to be as honest and realistic as you can.

Very Fearful   1   2   3   4   5   6   7   Not Fearful at all

APPLY   What did you learn this week that you found particularly comforting?

_____

_____

_____

_____

You may not be accustomed to thinking of Bible study application in this way, but a major point of application is simply thinking rightly. If we think wrongly about demons, we might be tempted to give them far too much credit—especially if we've seen how Hollywood depicts them.

What movies or television programs have you seen that have influenced your view of the demonic realm?

_____

_____

_____

_____

_____

_____

"Greater is He who is in you than he who is in the world"

1 John 4:4

APPLY Can you recognize any lies or exaggerations that this has fostered in your thinking?

_____

_____

_____

_____

_____

_____

Remember, the way to fight the father of lies is with truth. What is a specific verse or scriptural principle you need to stand on as you think about this area?

_____

_____

_____

_____

_____

_____

If you ever struggle with fear about the demonic realm, the answer is not to ignore it. The solution is God's truth. Hopefully this and the other lessons in this study will arm you with a better understanding of the power of God, the security of the believer, and the limitations of the devil and his demons. Why not close out this week's lesson by putting down on paper a prayer of trust and thanksgiving for God and His care of you.

_____

_____

_____

_____

_____

_____

_____

_____

_____

_____

_____

_____

Works Cited

1. _The Exorcist_ (film), Wikipedia, http://en.wikipedia.org/wiki/The_Exorcist.

2. _The Exorcist,_ Wikipedia, http://en.wikipedia.org/wiki/The_Exorcist.

3. Chad Garrison, "Hell of a House," Riverfront Times (October 26, 2005).

Notes

Notes

Notes

Notes

4

The World, the Flesh, and the Devil

The Federal Trade Commission estimates that as many as nine million Americans become victims of identity theft each year. The conventional wisdom has been that the offenders are strangers who collect personal information and then employ it. Sometimes they rummage through someone's trash until they find a name, social security number, credit card number, or other financial information. Another trick is "skimming" credit card data with a separate storage device while processing legitimate charges. Email scams called "phishing" pose as actual companies or financial institutions and use bogus inquiries to trick consumers into disclosing their personal information. Sometimes the purloined identity is nabbed the old-fashioned way—by stealing a wallet, lifting someone's mail, or snatching a purse. Using the victim's identifying information, the perpetrators can sign up for a credit card, set up a telephone account, or even rent an apartment. The thieves are long gone by the time their failure to pay works its way through the collection system. If you think about it long enough though, something doesn't add up. According to FBI statistics, there are about two million burglaries annually, and identity theft is a much more complicated crime. While the above-mentioned methods for stealing personal information are common, they probably aren't the primary way your identity is borrowed anymore. "You don't have ten million victims a year by people going through the trash," said one executive in an information security firm.[1]

Up to 70 percent of identity theft is an inside job.

According to research by Michigan State University, up to 70 percent of identity thefts are an inside job. The personal information of thousands of people is stolen at one time by the employee of a business where large quantities of personal information are held, such as a health care or financial institution. Consider an example from a recent FBI report. A former bank vice president was convicted of fraud involving the personal information of numerous clients. He apparently accepted bribes from questionable telemarketers and allowed them access to credit card information.[2] It makes perfect sense when you take time to think about it. Why steal identities one at a time when they can be stolen in mass quantities from corporate databases. Organizations of criminal minds target corporate America, costing business and ultimately their customers billions of dollars a year. Theft on such a grand scale is easy if the criminals have a person on the inside willing to cooperate with them. This is a good picture of the interplay between those who attack our devotion to Christ.

The devil is not omnipresent like the Lord. Just as it would be hard for one person to collect nine million identities a year by rummaging through trash, so Satan is limited because he cannot be everywhere at once. He doesn't have time to personally harass every believer. In fact, I doubt most believers will ever experience a personal visitation from Satan. This doesn't mean, however, that we are "off the hook" in spiritual battle. It just means that the devil will deal with most of us indirectly. He is able to do this, not only because of his legions of demons, but because he has some very powerful allies in his war with the Lord. The world system works with him, not the Lord. Most media outlets and even some of our educational entities promote agendas and ideologies that conflict with God and His Word. This, too, is part of spiritual warfare. If we stopped there, though, it would be easy to blame the devil and the world for all our sins and stumblings. As effective and impactful as they both are, part of our problem is an "inside job." There is something inside us—our flesh—that can be enticed to cooperate with the organized evil on the outside. The devil's attack and the world's pressure do not remove our personal responsibility for sin. This week we seek to understand the workings of this trilogy of enemies from a biblical perspective.

The World, the Flesh, and the Devil

DAY ONE

Did You Know?
WORLD

When Paul tells us not to be conformed to this world, the Greek word for "world" is not *kosmos* (the physical planet) but *aion*. This word connotes the present "age" in which we live.

THE WORLD AND THE DEVIL

When we speak of the dangers of the world, we aren't really speaking of this physical planet where we live. Rather, we are speaking of the world system—all the beliefs behind how our world normally runs that are not of God. Although it was founded on Christian principles, America is not a Christian nation. Christ and His Word do not dominate the halls of Congress or the corporate boardrooms. The dominant view of sexuality today is not a scriptural one. The entertainment industry of television, movies, and music is motivated by profit, not piety. Belief in the Creator's order is no longer the starting point in science education. Church is not only separate from the state; many seek to remove all vestiges of religion from public life. One of Satan's partners in this spiritual war we are in is the present world system.

Look up each of the verses below and record what they teach of Satan's relationship to the world in which we live.

📖 2 Corinthians 4:3–4 –

_____

_____

_____

📖 1 John 5:19 –

_____

_____

_____

📖 Ephesians 2:1–3 –

_____

_____

_____

Not only does Satan accomplish his purposes through his army of demons, but he also works through the conforming pressures of this world. Scripture teaches that he is the *"god of this world"* (2 Corinthians 4:4). In fact, 1 John 5:19 tells us that *"the whole world lies in the power of the evil one."* Satan has blinded the minds of those who will not believe (2 Corinthians 4:4). This is not saying that they cannot believe because Satan won't let them. Rather, their unbelief is because they choose not to believe. As a result, they have no defense against Satan's deceptions and he has them living a lie. Ephesians 2:2 reveals that *"the course of this world"* is *"according to the prince of the power of the air"* (Satan). That course is disobedience. Disobedience is rooted in the lie that our needs can be met apart from our Creator. That mindset is at the heart of all rebellion.

📖 What does 1 John 2:15–17 teach about the workings of this world system in drawing us away from the Lord?

_____

_____

_____

How does the world system work to instigate rebellion against God's will and way? The answer is found in 1 John 2:15–17. The key to the world's operation is the trio of the lust of the flesh (passions), the lust of the eyes (possessions), and the boastful pride of life (position). The lusts of the flesh obviously include the whole sexual arena, but we would be incorrect to limit it to that. In reality this includes everything that appeals to the senses—even food. There is nothing wrong with passion; God created it within us. But passion that is not surrendered to God's provision and timing becomes something that enslaves. The lust of the flesh is attempting to find fulfillment in pleasure, experiences, and indulgence instead of in Christ.

The lust of the eyes is that longing for everything I see. It is gluttony of possessions, thinking that if I have more, I will be happier. As with the lust of

The world system tempts us in three directions:
* *passions*
* *possessions*
* *positions*

the flesh, however, when we become unsatisfied with what God provides, we become a slave of the "more" monster, the never-fulfilled appetite for more things. The lust of the eyes is finding my fulfillment in what I possess and what those possessions do for me instead of in my relationship with Christ. This lust of the eyes may mean that I pick out my car, not based on what it does, but on how it looks to others and how much it costs. It can affect where and in what I live. America's love affair with credit cards is rooted in our unwillingness to wait for what God provides. Lust is always unwilling to wait on God.

The third facet of our world system's workings, the boastful pride of life, is being consumed with self and what self can do. This attitude is an inflated view of what man can accomplish without God. Whether those accomplishments are in business or in sports or in politics or even in religious activity, the operative word is "self." The boastful pride of life is finding our fulfillment in what we do instead of in what God does in and through us.

LOVING THE WORLD

As we saw yesterday in 1 John 2:15–17, John makes it clear that we are not to love the world. By this he does not mean the world itself, for God loves the people of the world (John 3:16). John's warning is against the world system that leaves God out and sets itself up as rival to Him. We are not to love the world system, nor are we to set our affections on the things of this world. God created us to love people and to make use of things. Satan inverts this and tries to draw us toward loving things and using people. Because ours is a fallen world, worldliness presents a real danger to the believer.

📖 Examine 2 Timothy 4:8 and 4:10 and examine the contrast there.

_____

_____

_____

_____

_____

"Demas, having loved this present world, has deserted me."

2 Timothy 4:10

In 2 Timothy 4:8 Paul instructs us that reward awaits those who *"loved His appearing."* Such an attitude involves trusting what God has promised regarding our future and valuing the next life more than the present one. In 2 Timothy 4:10 we discover that one of Paul's ministry companions was drawn away by worldliness. With sadness Paul expresses, *"Demas, having loved this present world, has deserted me."*

📖 Why, according to what you see in Hebrews 11:25, would someone be tempted to love the evil of this present world?

_____

_____

_____

Hebrews 11 recounts the great accomplishments wrought by faith during the Old Testament era. Verse 25 reminds us that there is a *"passing pleasure"* to sin. The world system constantly promotes that pursuit of gratification. Although the pleasure is there, it *is* passing, and the price tag is usually hidden. We learned in 1 John 2:17 that *"the world is passing away, along with its lusts."* A wise one looks beyond the immediate to what is ultimate.

📖 Reflect on James 4:4. What does this passage teach us about how God views the believer who becomes enamored with this world?

_____

_____

_____

With piercing insight, James equates friendship with the world with spiritual adultery. He asks, *"Do you not know that friendship with the world is hostility toward God?"* He goes on to say that *"whoever wishes to be a friend of the world makes himself an enemy of God."* Without reflection, we probably would not view this so negatively. Clearly the world system is an enemy of the believer. That is why the biblical writers make it clear that the followers of God are not to get too comfortable with the world. Peter calls us *"aliens"* (1 Peter 1:1), for this world is not our home. If this fallen world fits, then our faith must be the wrong size.

THE FLESH AND THE DEVIL

Why is the world so effective an enemy? If the main artillery of the world system is lust and pride, shouldn't our love of God keep us out of harm's way? The lies of this unredeemed realm should hold no temptation to the redeemed. One would think that the temporary trinkets that non-believers so cherish would be clearly seen as the cheap counterfeits they are when one has tasted of the goodness of the Lord. Yet experience affirms that we are not safe. Satan has another ally in this spiritual war in which we find ourselves. You see, all the schemes and deceptions of Satan and his demons, and all the conforming pressure of the world, would be of no avail were it not for the fact that there remains in us something that desires what they have to offer. The Bible identifies this adversary as our "flesh." God has not finished His reformation of our souls (see Philippians 1:6). Until He does, there will be a danger lurking in our own hearts.

📖 Meditate on Romans 7:21–23 and Galatians 5:16–17 and record what you learn there of the "flesh."

_____

_____

_____

_____

In Romans 7 Paul cautions us that there are within each of us evil desires that run counter to the law of God. These pagan passions within *"wage war"* against the truth we know. In Galatians 5 Paul emphatically affirms that our flesh sets its desire against the Spirit of God who lives in us. Flesh stands *"in opposition"* to God.

So what exactly is flesh? Flesh is that part of me that is not yet conformed to the image of Christ; that segment of my mind that has yet to be transformed by the renewing work of God's Word. Flesh is the portion of my will that is not fully surrendered to the Spirit's control. The term "flesh" points to those desires within me that are not the desires of God. Scripture describes two different manifestations of this principle—what I call bad flesh and good flesh. All that is fleshly is bad, but some fleshly behaviors are more culturally acceptable than others. "Bad flesh" is the term I apply to those behaviors that most everyone would label as wrong even though some choose to practice them. The deeds and attitudes that I identify as "good flesh" are those actions which appear good but flow from the pride of self. Another way of labeling them would be "rebellious flesh" and "religious flesh." Remember, it wasn't the drunkards and prostitutes who delivered Christ to be crucified. It was the religious leaders of the day whose own agendas and pride made them unable to see God in their midst.

📖 Write what you see in Galatians 5:19–21 of the fruit or deeds of the flesh.

_____

_____

_____

This list Paul gives to the Galatian believers is what I would call "bad flesh." Everything listed would be characterized as culturally unacceptable. When John spoke of the lust of the flesh and the lust of the eyes, he had actions such as these in mind.

Beyond these negative behaviors the apostle identifies, there also exists what I term "good flesh." I acknowledge that the phrase itself is a bit of an oxymoron, for there is no such thing as flesh that is good. There are, however, ways in which we wrongly view certain deeds as good even though the Bible labels them as flesh.

📖 Take a look at Matthew 7:22 and write down what you see there that could be considered "good flesh."

_____

_____

_____

"For I know that nothing good dwells in me, that is, in my flesh."

Romans 7:18

Clearly "good works" aren't good if Christ is not the author of them. When you think about it, this is a pretty radical concept. Doing the right thing isn't right if it doesn't flow out of a relationship with God. Flesh as the Bible describes it is what I do apart from God working in and through me. When I am immoral or have an outburst of anger, that is easily recognized as flesh. But when I strive to do good things in my own strength instead of by God's working in and through my life, then this too is flesh. The one is just as abhorrent to God as the other. As Isaiah put it, *"All our righteous deeds are like a filthy garment"* (Isaiah 64:6). In other words, man-centered righteousness isn't righteousness at all; it is just "good flesh." This is where the *"boastful pride of life"* comes in, for if I do a good deed on my own, Satan tempts me to take pride in it. But if God performs something positive through me, there is humility, because I recognize that all the glory should go to Him.

THE DEEDS OF THE FLESH

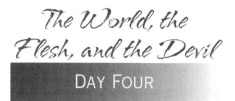

I n 1 Corinthians 3 Paul references a future judgment of believers' works. In 2 Corinthians 5:10 he calls this the *"judgment seat"* of Christ. This is not the judgment that determines whether a person's final destination is heaven or hell. The Bema judgment (so called because the Greek word for "judgment seat" is *bema*) is when the believer's works are judged with a view to reward. On that day, there will be a distinction drawn between what I have done for God in my own power and what God worked in and through me. What does this have to do with spiritual warfare, you may ask? A lot. Satan was the master of my flesh before I knew Christ. I didn't realize it then, but the entire unsaved world lies in his power. When I became a Christian, I got a new master. I don't have to serve the devil or my own fleshly desires anymore. Satan still barks orders at me, but I don't have to follow them anymore.

Part of the believer's struggle in warfare is this: if Satan can't get us entangled in "bad flesh" (immorality, sensuality, etc.), he has still succeeded if he can lure us into "good flesh" (doing seemingly good things in our own power and for our own glory). Once you get past the basics, the toughest decisions in the Christian life are no longer between good and bad. The toughest decisions we face as we mature are between that which is good and that which is God's will. This is where most of us struggle, and this too is a part of spiritual warfare. Satan wants to lead me astray from the simple, pure devotion that produces true fruit.

📖 Reflect on 1 Corinthians 3:10–11 and answer the questions below.

What is the foundation of the Christian life?

_____

_____

_____

Whose responsibility is it to build on that foundation?

_____

_____

_____

What attitude must the builder bring to the project?

_____

_____

_____

Employing an analogy, the apostle Paul pictures our Christian life as a building. He states emphatically that there can be only one foundation—

Did You Know?

THE JUDGMENT SEAT OF CHRIST

The Greek word for "judgment seat" (bema) referred to an elevated platform in each town, with an accompanying official chair, where judicial matters were decided. This judgment is different than the "Great White Throne" judgment where God the Father determines who goes to heaven and who goes to hell based on names written in the book of life (see Revelation 20:11–12).

Word Study
"BE CAREFUL"

Paul says that each person is to *"be careful"* how he builds upon the foundation of Christ. In the original text Paul used the Greek word *blepo*, the future tense of *optanomai* (from which we get "optics" and "optometrist"). This term literally means "to see." In other words, we should build with watchfulness. The expression is in the "imperative mood." This means that Paul's admonition is a command, not a suggestion.

Jesus Christ. We share in the responsibility of erecting upon that foundation a super-structure of spirituality. This building is not merely service, but would seem to include the fruit of Christian character (how we do what we do). We are commanded to take the task seriously.

Continue reading in 1 Corinthians 3 and from verses 12–15 record your observations to the following:

List the building materials Paul identifies in verse 12 and write your thoughts on how being tested by fire divides the list into categories.

_____

_____

_____

What are the possible results of this judgment of our deeds by fire?

_____

_____

_____

_____

What impact does this have on our salvation?

_____

_____

_____

As soon as you recognize that fire is the instrument of evaluation, the obvious distinction between the possible building materials is their flammability. The first three materials are not destroyed by fire. Instead, they are refined and purified. The last three are destroyed. The context of this passage is important. Paul began the chapter by contrasting the *"spiritual"* person with the *"fleshly"* believer. This distinction clarifies the later discussion of which effort produces a lasting reward. Jesus said, *"Apart from Me you can do nothing"* (John 15:5). On that day, what I performed on behalf of the Lord in my own strength will have amounted to *"wood, hay, [and] straw."* Because it was the product of the flesh, it will be burned to ashes in the judgment by fire. What God has accomplished through me is different. Those deeds will have produced *"gold, silver, [and] precious stones."* Such service and living will result in reward because it was initiated and empowered by the Spirit of God. If he can't get us into overt sin, Satan delights to draw us toward doing deeds *for* the Lord in our own strength.

According to James 1:14, who is to blame when we give in to sin?

_____

_____

_____

James makes it clear that if we aren't careful we might blame the external temptation for our sin instead of our own internal desires. Christ liberated me from being sin's slave. That doesn't mean I will never sin. It means I no longer have to. If I sin, it is always an inside job. Temptation is like the bait on the hook of a fisherman. It has two purposes: to heighten interest and to hide the hook. Bait does no good if it holds no interest for the fish, so it has to appeal to the fish's desires. Let's face it, you or I would have no interest at all in eating a worm, but to a bass it looks like filet mignon. Satan, the consummate fisherman, uses his demons and the world system to troll bait in front of us to try to lure us out of safety. God allows him to do this. Remember, it is not a sin to be tempted. The problem isn't the bait, it is the bite. The blame for the bite is not with Satan or his demons or the world or even the temptation. The blame for the bite lies with my own fleshly desires, whether they are bad flesh or even good flesh.

FOR ME TO FOLLOW GOD

The World, the Flesh, and the Devil
DAY FIVE

Some years ago the comedian Flip Wilson created a character named Geraldine who was always getting into trouble. Geraldine was a pastor's wife. When she had spent too much money on a new dress or when she had done something mean to a nosy neighbor, her explanation to her clerical husband was always, "The devil made me do it!" Satan is an easy target when we look for a place to lay blame other than with ourselves. This tendency is nothing new. With the very first sin in the garden, we see it in operation. When Adam was confronted with his guilt for eating the forbidden fruit, his explanation was, *"The woman whom Thou gavest…gave me from the tree"* (Genesis 3:12). With one statement he tries to deflect some of the blame for his own choice onto both Eve and God. Eve does the same thing. She blames the serpent for deceiving her. As humorous as the character Geraldine was, her attitude is no laughing matter to many believers. If we are not careful, pride can creep in and make us unwilling to recognize our own responsibility for sin. We might sometimes find ourselves blaming the devil, his demons, and the temptations of this fallen world instead of acknowledging our own flesh.

In Romans 12:2 Paul makes an imperative statement to believers: *"Do not be conformed to this world."* One of the ways the world system exerts pressure on us to conform is through the people around us—the standards they set for what is acceptable, what is popular, and what is important. What are some ways you experience that pressure to conform in the areas below?

Music –

_____

_____

Movies/Television –

_____

_____

_____

"And do not be conformed to this world, but be transformed by the renewing of your mind."

Romans 12:2

Clothing –

_____

_____

_____

Possessions –

_____

_____

_____

Values –

_____

_____

_____

Priorities –

_____

_____

_____

In order to recognize the lies of this world system that is manipulated by the "god of this world," we must be equipped with truth. Paul goes on in Romans 12:2 to contrast conforming to the world with being *"transformed by the renewing of your mind."* We need a new way of thinking in each area so that what we think is shaped by God's Word instead of the world's values. In the list above, pick one area where you feel the greatest conforming pressure. Plan a time to research what God's word has to say about this area, so you can allow your mind to be renewed to what God wants it to be. If you need some help coming up with verses, ask mature Christians you know.

The area I want to address first:

_____

_____

_____

_____

When I plan to do this (give yourself a deadline):

_____

_____

_____

_____

The world in which we live is fallen. Because of this, each of us has been influenced by world views that differ from God's way. Consider the many philosophical "isms" of our time and identify which have influenced you the most or give you trouble.

____ Relativism (there are no absolutes)
____ Sensualism (fulfillment is in pleasure)
____ Humanism (effort can solve everything)
____ Fatalism (nothing we do really matters)
____ Materialism (fulfillment is in possessions)
____ Rationalism (all is explained naturally)
____ Spiritism (there are many competing gods)
____ Other:_____

Sin usually falls into one of two categories. Some violations are crimes of **commission**. We commit specific acts that are wrong. Other offenses are sins of **omission**. This is when the transgression isn't what we do that we shouldn't, but is in what we don't do that we should. All sins are sins of **submission**. They are enthronements of our own will over the will of God. Some may be unintentional, but occur because we act without first listening to God's instruction.

APPLY What are some "bad flesh" sins that tempt you? (Be honest. You may want to answer in some private code if you fear these notes will be seen by others.)

_____

_____

_____

_____

_____

APPLY Understanding the concept of "good flesh," can you see any examples of it in your own walk?

_____

_____

_____

_____

Romans 13:14 provides a very practical battle plan for protecting ourselves from our own flesh, the world, and the devil. Paul writes, *"Put on the Lord Jesus Christ, and make no provision for the flesh in regard to its lusts."*

To "make provision" for our flesh means doing things that make it easy for us to fall in the future. If clothing catalogs make it easy for you to covet, call and ask to be taken off the mailing list. If television programs tempt you, get rid of cable or block offending channels. If overeating is a problem, get an accountability partner (and don't window shop at the candy store). If the internet is causing you to stumble, buy a filter program and let someone else operate the password. Paul is saying that in the spiritual battle for our devotion to Christ, we need help. We need to arrange our lives to make it harder to fall when we are weak. What are some changes you need to effect in order to make no provision for your flesh and its lusts?

_____

_____

_____

"Put on the Lord Jesus Christ, and make no provision for the flesh in regard to its lusts."

Romans 13:14

_____

_____

_____

_____

The other solution Paul offers is to put on the Lord Jesus Christ. We "put on" Christ when we yield every area of our lives to His control. It starts by simply telling Him we desire Him to rule that area instead of us. As we close out this week's lesson, why don't you write out a prayer that puts this desire into your own words.

_____

_____

_____

_____

_____

_____

_____

_____

_____

_____

Works Cited

1. Bob Sullivan, "Study: ID theft usually an inside job," MSNBC (May 21, 2004), http://www.msnbc.com/id/5015565.

2. "FBI Financial Institution Fraud and Failure Report 2003," 37, http://www.fbi.gov/publications/financial/2003fif/fif03.pdf m/id/5015565.

Notes

Notes

5

The Believer's Defense

What do you think of when you hear the word "defense?" Your answer is probably shaped in great measure by your own interests and experiences. Athletes and sports fans are likely to view the term from that perspective. Their minds run to efforts aimed at preventing the other player or team from victory. A criminal or an attorney thinks of avoiding a conviction. While both of those concepts are relevant, our study applies the term in the context of war. In military applications the expression is usually employed in reference to protecting a country or territory from enemy attack. A defensive military strategy aims to prevent an attack or to minimize the opponent's chance of success. When one is in defensive mode, the concern isn't with taking new territory, but with protecting what is already owned. In ancient times cities defended themselves to some degree by moats and walls. Frontier forts would erect a fence and clear trees away from the barricade to prevent an unseen assault. To counter such tactics, the battle plan of a marauding army often involved "laying siege" to a settlement. Invaders would endeavor to cut off supplies to the city and try to starve them out rather than experience excessive casualties trying to penetrate established defenses.

Throughout history, the advantage in war lies with the defenders more than the attackers. The aggressors must abandon their positions, making themselves vulnerable as they seek to capture new ground. The guardians of a city can and should prepare for an attack before one is encountered. They can take advantage of

If we desire success in this spiritual conflict, we must understand the keys of our defense.

assets such as higher ground, natural barriers, and man-made obstacles for greater protection. If they are able to anticipate a battle, they can arrange their position with trenches and fortifications. When it comes to defense, the solution is preparation.

This is equally true in spiritual warfare. The world, the flesh and the devil have conspired to lead us astray from *"the simplicity and purity of devotion to Christ"* (2 Corinthians 11:3). If we desire success in this spiritual conflict, we must understand the keys of our defense.

If you have any doubt that "war" is a suitable description for the conflict between the forces of God and the forces of Satan, there are two verses of Scripture that should settle the question. The apostle Paul wrote to the Corinthian church, *"For the weapons of our* **warfare** *are not of the flesh, but divinely powerful for the destruction of fortresses"* (2 Corinthians 10:4, emphasis mine). To the Ephesian believers he made it clear, *"Our struggle is not against flesh and blood, but against the rulers, against the powers, against the world forces of this darkness, against the* **spiritual** *forces of wickedness in the heavenly places"* (Ephesians 6:12, emphasis mine). The legitimacy of spiritual warfare is not a debatable issue in the body of Christ; God's Word makes it clear that there is a war. The real issue is in defining its priorities and parameters. Practices employed in parts of the body of Christ today far exceed the constraints related in the Scriptures. The techniques being applied by some believers give the subject of warfare greater priority than is Biblically modeled or seems logically prudent. There is equal danger, however, of reacting to the imbalance of some by dismissing the subject altogether. There are those who do not mention spiritual warfare for fear of being misunderstood. Both extremes are wrong. Our goal should not be extremes but a move toward balance.

The Believer's Defense

THE PREEMINENT RULE OF GOD

Understanding what the Bible teaches about spiritual warfare is crucial to finding the needed balance. Since believers are caught in the crossfire of this spiritual conflict, a first issue to address is, what defense is available? What assistance can I call upon so that I am not devoured by this "roaring lion" called Satan? A vital truth to identify is that the believer's defense does not begin with the believer—it begins with God. He is *all* that we need for any circumstance. All that He is comes to our aid in the arena of spiritual warfare. God the Father, God the Son, and God the Holy Spirit are all involved in our spiritual defense. Psalm 28:8 expresses it this way: *"The Lord is their strength, and He is a saving defense to His anointed."* We will begin this lesson by looking at what the Scriptures teach about the Lord as our defense. Our enemy, Satan, is *"like a roaring lion, seeking someone to devour,"* but he is a lion on a leash. Only God is pre-eminent. He was, is, and always will be in control. Because He is *omnipotent* (all-powerful), *omniscient* (all-knowing), and *omnipresent* (ever-present), Satan is under His authority. From looking at Job we learned that Satan reports to God (Job 1:6; 2:1). We saw that God set the boundaries of Satan's attacks on Job (Job 1:12, 2:6). It is reassuring to know that the adversary can only go as far as God allows.

You may ask, "Why does God allow Satan to go anywhere at all?" If our Lord has the power to get rid of Lucifer, why doesn't He go ahead and do it? Scripture doesn't give us an answer to that question; it only assures us that God's purposes are always right and for our benefit. We must factor God's omniscience into our assessment. Since He is all-knowing, He knew before Satan was created that he would rebel. God would never have brought him into existence if his rebellion did not somehow fit in our Lord's purposes. Revelation 20:1 tells us that all it takes to throw Satan into the abyss is one angel and God's command. When God's intended purpose is complete, He will only have to speak the word. It is a great comfort to realize that the Lord is able to use even Satan's actions for our benefit and His glory. That was exemplified in the life of Job.

📖 Reflect on 2 Corinthians 12:7–9 to learn how God uses the devil in Paul's life for good, and answer the questions that follow.

What was the reason for the "thorn" in Paul's flesh?

_____

_____

_____

Where did this "thorn" originate?

_____

_____

_____

To whom did Paul address his request for its removal?

_____

_____

_____

APPLY What can you glean from God's response to Paul?

_____

_____

_____

The most obvious character in this passage is the *"messenger of Satan."* Who or what is this? Some say it was a demon, for the Greek word for *"messenger"* (*aggelos*) is the term for an angel. It must be noted, however, that any messenger —human, angelic, or otherwise—can fit the meaning of this particular word. It is not an expression reserved for angelic beings. It can and often does refer to human messengers. It seems unlikely that *"thorn"* should be taken literally. Rather, it appears to represent some person, trial, or affliction. Any attempt to identify it as a demon would be unsupportable conjecture. Paul refers to this thorn as a *"weakness."* In so doing, he hints at some area of personal struggle. Perhaps it was a person the Lord used to reveal Paul's weakness. If we take this encounter to mean a demon, the resulting ramifications to spiritual warfare are significant.

"If God is for us, who is against us?"

Romans 8:31

 *Word Study*
THORN

The Greek word for thorn (*skolops*) does not mean a tiny briar that pricks your finger. That Greek term is *akantha* (e.g. Jesus' crown of thorns in Matthew 27:29). The word used here means a sharpened wooden staff, or a stake used for impaling or torturing someone. The use of this word emphasizes the sharpness of the object and its capability to cause great pain.

We learn from Paul in this passage that the *"thorn"* was something the Lord did not want to remove. Rather, it served as a means of causing Paul to depend on God's grace instead of his own strength. For Paul, this painful circumstance became an object of boasting. If indeed this thorn was a demon, why was God unwilling to grant Paul's request for removal? Why would Paul boast in such an infirmity? It seems more likely that it was some spiritual or physical affliction. Whatever its identity, the thorn was from Satan. At the same time, Paul's thorn in the flesh was used to accomplish the Lord's purpose, and He would not remove it. In our own struggles with the enemy, we would do well to remember that the Lord is in control.

Paul's response to Satan's thorn affords us a good model. Notice that he did not rebuke the messenger of Satan. He did not bind him or charge him to do anything in Jesus' name—he didn't even speak to him! He simply prayed to the Lord. Even when Satan attacks us, our focus is not to be on him. Rather, we are to fix our eyes on Jesus. There are some today who teach that we have the authority to make the devil do what we command. It is interesting to note that Paul did not get the answer he wanted. Even though he was an apostle, this position of great authority in the church did not give him the right to "claim" victory or healing, or to command Satan to do what he desired. The faith-life dictates that in spiritual warfare we must not fight the battle ourselves. We must let Jesus fight for us as we yield to Him. A sissy demon could whip you or me any day of the week, but the mightiest demon of all is no match for the Almighty.

Do you recall how the legion of demons possessing the man in the country of the Gerasenes reacted when they encountered Jesus?

_____

_____

_____

📖 Look again at Mark 5:1–13. What difference do you see between what people are able to do with the legion of demons and what Christ is able to do?

_____

_____

_____

In Mark 5:4 we are told that *"no one was strong enough to subdue him."* Not even chains and shackles could hold this demon-possessed person. Yet these same demons tremble in the presence of Christ. The demons begged Jesus for permission to go into a herd of pigs. Notice what verse 13 says of Jesus' response: *"Jesus gave them permission."* Even a legion of demons is no match for the Lord. It ought to encourage us to realize that our protection doesn't start with ourselves. Our defense begins with the pre-eminent rule of God.

Who is in control of our temptations? Is it Satan, or does God have the final say? Look at 1 Corinthians 10:13 and write what you learn there of God's role in Satan's temptations of us.

_____

_____

_____

I consider this one of the greatest promises of Scripture. Yet the truth of this verse is impossible apart from the sovereign rule of God. Our Heavenly Father expresses His faithfulness to us by not allowing us to be tempted beyond what we are able to bear. In other words, my temptations and trials are tailor-made for me. Each is first reviewed by the Lord, who ensures I am able before He allows it. If God, in His infinite knowledge, determines something is more than I am able to bear, He prevents it. Because of this, no matter how intense the battle with sin, I can never say that I am incapable of overcoming. There is always a promised way of escape. Looking at the Bible as a whole, we see that Jesus is the way of escape, regardless of the problem. Whatever a demon is capable of, one thing he cannot do is put a Christian in a place where he cannot do right, where he cannot obey, where he cannot return to the Lord. God's sovereignty guarantees this.

THE PRESENT WORK OF CHRIST

When Christ died on the cross, He satisfied the payment necessary for our sins for all time. Hebrews 7:27 instructs us that payment for our sins was made *"once for all when He offered up Himself."* When our Lord rose from the dead, He conquered death. Paul called Him *"the first fruits"* from the dead (1 Corinthians 15:20). We learn in Hebrews 9:11–12 that Christ entered into the true Tabernacle in heaven and sprinkled His own blood on that heavenly Mercy Seat. When these indispensable works were completed, *"having offered one sacrifice for sins for all time,"* the Lord Jesus Christ *"sat down at the right hand of God, waiting from that time onward until His enemies be made a footstool for His feet"* (Hebrews 10:12–13). These are glorious words indeed, but do not wrongly interpret Christ's present seated posture. He is not idle, nor is He inactive. While He waits for Satan and his co-rebels to be put down, He is also working. Today we want to focus on the present work of Christ and its impact on spiritual warfare.

📖 Reflect on Hebrews 7:25 and record what you learn of Christ's ministry to and for us right now.

_____

_____

_____

What an awesome reminder that Jesus is praying for you and me right now! We are never left unguarded. We always have the attention of heaven. Paul wrote to the Roman believers, *"Christ Jesus is He who died, yes, rather who was raised, who is at the right hand of God, who also intercedes for us"* (Romans 8:34). When you face spiritual attack, never forget there is a constant conversation in the throne room of God on your behalf.

Write how you see this intercessory work of Christ modeled in John 17:15.

_____

_____

_____

Did You Know?
TEMPTATIONS AND TRIALS

In English translations of Scripture, both words come from forms of the same Greek word.

The Believer's Defense

DAY TWO

> ## "Christ Jesus is He who died, yes, rather who was raised, who is at the right hand of God, who also intercedes for us"
>
> ### Romans 8:34

We see an example of Jesus' intercessory work as He prays for the disciples in Gethsemane. Notice that He doesn't ask the Father to remove them from the environment of danger, but rather to protect them in that environment. It is a subtle but significant distinction—He works for your victory, but not that you would avoid the battle. In whatever spiritual conflict you encounter, you can rest assured that Jesus is praying for you.

How do you see the intercessory work of Jesus illustrated with Peter in Luke 22:31–32?

_____

_____

_____

It is worth noticing, first of all, that Jesus prays for Peter. In fact, it isn't just that Christ was praying for Peter as the devil sifted him. Christ said, *"I have prayed for you."* His intercessory work began even before the difficulty was encountered. Equally telling is what He prays and what He does not pray. Jesus does not pray that Satan be bound and banished, nor does He rebuke Satan or pray a hedge of protection around Peter. Instead, He prays that Peter's faith would not fail. And the implication of the last part of the verse is that Jesus already knew it would not. Jesus was concerned that Peter pass the test, not that He avoid it.

The Believer's Defense

DAY THREE

THE PROTECTIVE ARMOR OF CHRIST

At the end of lesson three I shared the story of a close encounter I had with an 8–foot shark while spearfishing in the Bahamas. One realization that drove my fear in that encounter was a clear sense of my own vulnerability. The smallest species of shark has jaws bigger than the largest species of dog. The power of a shark to do physical harm to a person is great. While humans can do nothing to decrease the power and capabilities of sharks, there are remedies that decrease individual vulnerability. A "shark cage" is often employed by those working in close proximity to dangerous sharks. Of course, it is not the shark that is placed in the cage, but the human. Another method of personal protection is a "chain mail suit." You may be familiar with the chain mail armor used by knights in medieval times. Interlocking metal rings made the armor more flexible than traditional solid armor. This gave the soldier much more freedom of movement, while still providing protection from swords and arrows. That same concept has been revived today and applied in certain underwater situations. For the small price of $23,000, you can buy the "Neptunic C Suit" made from steel mesh, high tech fiber, titanium, and hybrid laminates. This product is made for underwater use and prevents a shark's teeth from penetrating. If the shark is big enough, however, it could still cause pain, bruising, and even broken bones.

The promise of the high–tech shark suit is that any damage done in such an attack would be far less than if the swimmer weren't wearing the suit.[1] The same could be said for any kind of armor. One of the protections a Christian has in spiritual battle is *"the full armor of God."* Ephesians 6 introduces the believer to this protection in Christ. Since there is armor available that can provide us a measure of protection against the attacks of the enemy, we should be motivated to learn how to obtain and use this protective covering. That will be our focus in today's study.

📖 Review Ephesians 6:14–17 and make a list of each component of the *"full armor of God"* that you find cataloged there. With each article, summarize what you think that means practically in the spiritual realm.

_____

_____

_____

_____

_____

As with any portion of Scripture, we must remind ourselves that the truth is expressed in a cultural and historical frame. The author was writing at a specific point in time and within a specific cultural context. To rightly interpret the intended meaning, we must view what is written through that historical and cultural lens. When Paul writes of military armor, no doubt he is assuming the reader will picture in his mind the normal outfitting of a Roman soldier. This fact is helpful in understanding the pieces he lists.

Paul's analogy of the *"full armor of God"* begins with *"having girded your loins with truth."* A Roman soldier's sword was connected to his belt for quick and easy access. It was the one piece of armor a soldier wore at all times. Likewise, a Christian must always be girded with truth – not just having it available, but having it secured and accessible as with a belt. Next comes the *"breastplate of righteousness."* An injury to the chest was often fatal, so this vital area was protected in battle. In a practical sense, righteousness is a protection against personal damage. Paul then mentions feet: *"having shod your feet with the preparation of the gospel of peace."* While it is certainly true that Christians ought to be prepared to share the gospel, the reference to the feet should be viewed in the context of the repeated admonition to "stand." Since Roman solders wore studded shoes for better footing in battle, the implication seems to be that a right view of the gospel gives us stability. After that, we are to take up the *"shield of faith"* and the *"helmet of salvation."* Both of these pieces are pretty self-explanatory. Finally, Paul identifies the *"sword of the Spirit"* as our offensive weapon. He interprets for us that this is the word of God.

Most Bibles will have certain phrases from this passage in all capital letters. This means they are quoted from the Old Testament. If your Bible has a "cross-reference" feature, look at Ephesians 6:14–17 and identify the Old Testament sources of these quotes. Write these down along with your thoughts on what they mean. If your Bible doesn't have cross-references, don't worry. I'll give those to you. However, there is power in seeing things for yourself instead of being spoon-fed. By completing the exercises before you read on, you are not only experiencing the joy of self-discovery, but you also have the added benefit of learning Bible study techniques you can use elsewhere.

_____

_____

_____

_____

Did You Know?
THE OUTFITTED ROMAN SOLDIER

The personal armor of a Roman soldier changed over time. The chest was protected by either the *lorica hamata* (a chain mail shirt), the *lorica segmentata* (overlapping broad plates of armor), or the *lorica squamata* (inter-connected scales of armor). The *scutum* was the Roman version of a shield. Each warrior was outfitted with a military belt (called *cingulum*) designed to hold his *pugio* (a small dagger) and *gladius* (a short sword). Select soldiers were outfitted with spears (a *hasta* or *pilum*). On the fighter's feet were *caligae*, shoes with studded soles much like modern athletic cleats. A helmet called the *galea* protected the combatant's cheeks, ears and neck.

As we do a thorough exegesis of this passage, we find that the armor mentioned here all appears in Isaiah (11:4–5, 49:2, 52:7, 59:17) in passages prophesying the Messiah. So in a very tangible sense, when we put on Christ, we put on the armor.

In Ephesians 6:14 the command to *"take your stand"* or *"stand firm"* is in the Aorist Active Imperative, which means this is the main point of the passage. The other verbs (*"having girded"*, *"having put on"*, *"having shod"*) all appear in the Aorist Middle Particle, which because of their temporal relationship to the main verb, indicate action prior to that of the main verb (thus the NAS translates it in the past tense). The Middle voice tells us that it is we who place these pieces of armor on ourselves to stand firm. Thus we put on all of the armor of God in order that we may be able to *"stand firm."*

 What is it that we are instructed to do in order to put on the armor?

_____

_____

_____

Word Study
TAKE

In Ephesians 6:16 we are told to be *"taking up the shield of faith."* In the next verse we are told to *"take the helmet of salvation."* There is an interesting change of pattern when we get to verse 17. Rather than using the same word he used in verse 16 for *"taking"* (*analambano*), Paul uses a different word for *"take"* the helmet of salvation (*dechomai*), which literally means "receive."

It appears to me that these essential pieces of protection (the girded loins, the breastplate of righteousness, the shod feet) are permanently in place at salvation. How, if Christ is my righteousness, is it possible for me to remove my righteousness? One might say "by unrighteous deeds," but that would mean that it is my uprightness and morality rather than Christ's. Since Christ is my righteousness and He will neither leave me nor forsake me (Heb. 13:5), then my vital organs are always protected. Likewise, my salvation, which is my helmet, protects my head from fatal blows. Again the question arises, "If salvation is our helmet, how can we take it off?" It is my opinion that the essential aspects of my protection are in place when I clothe myself with Christ. An important part of the believer's defense is the fact that he is in Christ.

In order to complete my armor I must take up my shield, which I do by walking in the faith, and use my sword, the *"word"* (*rhema*) of God, which is the specific Scriptures the Holy Spirit reminds me of in my time of need (see John 14:26). When Paul speaks of the *"shield of faith,"* the word "faith" appears in the Greek with the definite article. This means he is referring not to faith in general (the principle of faith), but to a specific faith ("THE faith"). Usually this means the tenets of the Christian faith and is synonymous with walking with God in sound doctrine. In addition, I do battle when I pray. Verses 18–20 indicate that it too is part of spiritual warfare.

📖 Look at Romans 13:12–14 and write what you learn there about putting on the armor.

_____

_____

_____

_____

The "armor of God" does not represent a series of disjointed truths. Rather, it presents one truth: Christ.

We are called to *"put on the armor of light."* The passage also indicates that is what we do that when we *"put on the Lord Jesus Christ."* The armor is not a mystical possession; it is a person—our Savior.

Although many teach putting on the armor as an extra step in the Christian life, there is no Biblical substantiation for "praying on the armor" piece by piece as a daily exercise. I put on Christ when I became a Christian. I put the armor on when I put on Christ (yield myself to His control and Lordship in every area of my life). Paul uses these parts as metaphors to help us visualize our protection in Christ. We do a real disservice to Ephesians chapter 6 when we separate it from the rest of the book of Ephesians, yet few of us have really taken the time to understand it in that context. The central theme of the entire book of Ephesians is who we are in Christ. Viewed in this light, the analogy of *"armor of God,"* found in chapter 6 does not represent a series of disjointed truths. Rather, it presents one truth: Christ. Therefore, I do not believe that the armor should be viewed as individual pieces, but as parts of a whole.

You Are Not Alone

I don't think any one of us relishes the idea of fighting a spiritual war. We want to see the kingdom of God progress, but we would prefer that its advancement be without opposition. That isn't the case. As you reflect on spiritual warfare, I am confident you are encouraged to remember that God is the Almighty—no enemy is His equal. I trust you are comforted with the knowledge that Christ has an ongoing prayer ministry on your behalf. I hope you feel more secure with a better understanding of the armor of God. As great a blessing as these three protections are for Christians engaged in spiritual conflict, the defense of the believer doesn't end there. Our study this day will focus on two additional assets that are yours because you are His.

📖 What does Galatians 5:16 teach is the safeguard against sin?

_____

_____

_____

It is the empowering work of the Spirit of God that guards me from giving in to my fleshly desires. I cannot consistently say no to the flesh on my own. I must be directed and empowered by the Spirit, and for this to happen, I must maintain my fellowship with God. How do I stay in a right relationship with the Lord? I keep my walk healthy by keeping short accounts with God about my sin as the Spirit convicts me. I stay spiritually strong as I yield every area of my life to His control. When my life is empowered and directed by the Holy Spirit, He is able to be through me everything that I cannot be in my own strength.

📖 What are we commanded to do in Ephesians 5:18?

_____

_____

_____

Here in the same context as the armor of God, we are commanded to *"be filled with the Spirit."* To be filled with the Spirit does not mean that you need

> *"But encourage one another day after day, as long as it is still called 'Today,' so that none of you will be hardened by the deceitfulness of sin."*
>
> **Hebrews 3:13**

to get more of the Holy Spirit. It means that He needs to get more of you. The Spirit of God needs to be allowed access to every area of your life. Each part must be placed under His management and kept that way. As it is a command, we know that this call to be filled is God's will. Since God would not ask us to do something beyond our ability, we know that we are able to do it. Practically speaking, being filled with the Spirit is the same thing as "putting on the Lord Jesus." It means yielding control of our lives to God.

What does this mean for you in spiritual warfare? Part of your defense is that you never have to face any fray by yourself. Whether it involves battling temptation or standing strong against opposition, no conflict with the enemy need be entered alone. But there is more.

📖 According to Hebrews 3:13, what is the responsibility of the Church for believers in spiritual battle?

_____

_____

_____

The Church of Jesus Christ is not a collection of individuals. The Bible teaches that we are all members of one body. When one part hurts, we all hurt. When one part is endangered, we all are being challenged. We all need to take responsibility for one another and seek to keep each other encouraged. This is where Christian fellowship enters the picture. We are much easier targets for the enemy when we are alone than when we are together.

📖 How does Hebrews 10:24–25 teach that we fulfill this God-given responsibility?

_____

_____

_____

_____

God's Word always tells us how to do what God desires. We should be thinking up ways to stimulate one another toward love and good deeds. Most importantly, we must assemble together. As our Lord's return draws nearer, we need even more to come together and encourage one another. I am reminded of Ben Franklin's address to the continental congress as they prepared to declare their independence from Great Britain: "We must all hang together, or assuredly we shall all hang separately." We need to "hang together" as Christians. We need to regularly be involved in a local church and in relationships with other believers. This is part of our defense. Making this a reality is an individual responsibility. Each of us must connect to a local body where we can be encouraged and help other believers. Several logs burn brightly when they are close together in a fire, but if you take one log and isolate it, the flames die down quickly. While we should take personal ownership of our call to fellowship with other believers, this is also a responsibility of the church. Each church must connect its people in relationship so that someone knows if another isn't there. As the body of Christ, we must seek out those who are trying to go it alone, lest they become prey of the enemy.

FOR ME TO FOLLOW GOD

It is said of many sports that championships are won on defense. We need to realize that when it comes to spiritual warfare, we have a tremendous defense. We are undergirded with the preeminent rule of God. When we encounter the accuser of the brethren, and even before, we are covered by the present intercessory work of Christ. We are protected by the armor of Christ. We needn't worry about being overpowered in our conflicts with our adversary, for the power of the Holy Spirit is available to us. As we stand our ground, we do not stand alone. The people of God stand with us. As comforting as it is to be reminded of the strength of our defense in strife with our enemy, there is one more aspect of a Christian's defense to consider.

APPLY In Day Three we looked at Romans 13:14 in its context. Review it again and then write down what you think it means to "make provision for your flesh."

_____

_____

_____

Consider your own walk with Christ, and identify any areas of vulnerability where you might be making provision for your own weaknesses.

_____

_____

_____

What changes do you sense you need to make?

_____

_____

_____

I need to regularly examine my life, especially areas of personal struggle, and ask myself, "Am I doing anything to make it easier on the devil?" Perhaps I need to get rid of cable TV, or change my choice of music. Maybe I need to be more selective in choosing friends. We do not need to answer these questions alone. We should ask the Lord to reveal any places where we are providing for our own failure by making provision for our flesh. We should also ask for His direction in how to address these vulnerabilities.

When we talk about spiritual warfare, it sounds like we are looking for a fight. When we must, we should fight with all our might, but that isn't our only option. Sometimes we try to fight a temptation because we overestimate our own strength. A second part of our personal responsibility in spiritual defense is to learn to flee. In the Scriptures we find repeated exhortations to "flee" rather than to fight.

In 1 Corinthians 6:18 we are exhorted, *"Flee immorality."*

> **We should ask the Lord to reveal any places where we are providing for our own failure by making provision for our flesh.**

In 1 Corinthians 10:14 we read, *"Flee from idolatry."*

In 1 Timothy 6:10–11 Paul says,

The love of money is a root of all sorts of evil, and some by longing for it have wandered away from the faith, and pierced themselves with many griefs. **But flee from these things, you man of God**, *and pursue righteousness, godliness, faith, love perseverance and gentleness."* (emphasis mine)

This same theme is picked up in 2 Timothy 2:22, where Paul admonishes Timothy, *"Now flee from youthful lusts, and pursue righteousness, faith, love and peace, with those who call upon the Lord from a pure heart."*

APPLY Can you think of examples in Scripture, in your own experience, or in that of others, where fleeing wasn't pursued and stumbling was the result?

_____

_____

_____

_____

_____

So what is my defense in spiritual warfare? Review your notes with a view to any actions or attitudes that need to change in your walk. Check the areas below where you feel change needs to happen to make the most of your defense.

____ The pre-eminent rule of the Father   ____ The present work of Christ
____ The protective armor of Christ   ____ The power of the Spirit
____ The people of God   ____ Making no provision for the flesh.

Why don't you conclude the considerations of this week by writing out your heart-felt supplications to the Lord.

_____

_____

_____

_____

_____

_____

_____

_____

"Now flee from youthful lusts, and pursue righteousness, faith, love and peace, with those who call upon the Lord from a pure heart."

2 Timothy 2:22

Works Cited

1. Frank Walker, "Swim With Sharks in Bite-Proof Suit," *The Age.com* (December 30, 2007), http://www.smh.com.au/news/national/swim-with-sharks-in-biteproof-suit/2007/12/29/1198778769208.html

Notes

Notes

Notes

6

The Believer's Offense

The traditional view in sports and in warfare is that the advantage lies with the one on defense, but this is not always the case. There are some advantages in being the one who initiates the attack. For one thing, the aggressor chooses the time and place of battle. In addition, an attacker may concentrate his entire army on a small part of the defended area, while the defender is forced to spread his troops over every possible area of attack. We see how these factors relate when the devil is on the offensive with us. But is there any place where we can go on the offensive? Not in the sense that Satan does. We do not lie in ambush for the adversary. Deception has no place in the believer's arsenal. The only ground we seek to take is the hearts of those our enemy holds captive. That being said, the role of the Christian is not merely to sit back and wait for the next onslaught.

Perhaps the most important subject in our discussion of spiritual warfare is the how a believer should respond to the devil. What is our offensive response? Only a handful of passages specifically address how the believer is to counter Satan. To gain a Biblical understanding of the believer's response, we will look at each of these passages and try to identify the common denominators. The main passages are 1 Peter 5:5b–9, Ephesians 6:10–18, and James 4:6–10. There are also other relevant passages that address the subject in an indirect way, and we will look at some of them. These three passages, however, are the most specific in Scripture directly addressing how the believer is

The main New Testament passages addressing the topic of spiritual warfare are:

1 Peter 5:5b–9
Ephesians 6:10–18
James 4:6–10

to respond in spiritual warfare. A further benefit is that they give us the viewpoint of three different authors: Peter, James, and Paul. These three are undoubtedly among the most significant men of the early church. Peter was the most prominent of the twelve disciples of Jesus. James, the brother of Jesus, was the recognized leader of the Mother Church in Jerusalem. Paul was the leading missionary of the day and authored most of the New Testament. Together they represent the prominent theological minds of the early days of the Christian faith.

The Believer's Offense

DAY ONE

THE BIG PICTURE

Each of these warfare passages presents a unique vantage point from which to view the subject of the believer's response to the devil. But they share some common themes as well. It is these commonalities that speak loudest, and their repetition in Scripture emphasizes their importance. Since these three passages represent the most specific teaching on how we are to respond to the devil, I think it is safe to conclude that the truths common to all three passages are the essence of spiritual warfare. If you are at all like me, you will be surprised to discover what is included on this list, and just as surprised at what is left off of the list. But if we are to be biblical in our practice, we must major on what Scripture views as most important, and we must be willing to lay aside any practices that are not based on Scripture, no matter how popular they are. Let's dig into the Word and see what we find.

Briefly read each of the three passages listed below and then record what similarities you observe between them (common words and ideas).

📖 1 Peter 5:5b–9, Ephesians 6:10–18, James 4:6–10

_____

_____

_____

_____

"**Submit therefore to God. Resist the devil and he will flee from you. Draw near to God and He will draw near to you.**"

James 4:7–8a

As we overview these passages, we see several ideas that appear in two of the three. We will look at these later in the study. Only one idea shows up in all three passages. It is the word *"resist."* What does it mean to resist? *Webster's Dictionary* offers two possibilities:
1. to withstand; fend off
2. to oppose actively; fight against.

That is how we use the term in English, but the Bible wasn't written in English. If we want to understand what the biblical writers meant, we need to study the Greek word they used. Paul, James, and Peter used the same word: *anthistemi.* It actually is a compound expression formed from two Greek words, *anti*, meaning "against," and *histemi*, meaning "to stand." This is significant, for clearly the implication of the word is not that I chase after Satan. Rather, to resist the devil means that I hold my ground against his efforts, and I do not allow Satan to pull me away from where I stand. The difference is subtle but significant. Practically speaking, "resisting" the devil means that when he tries to pull me away from my secure standing place—being rightly related to the Lord—I just say "No!"

As amazing as it seems, James states quite clearly that all it takes to send the devil running is to resist him. No incantations are required, no formula prayers are necessary, no rebukes are needed. All we have to do, James says, is *"resist the devil and he will flee from you."* Actually, what I just said really isn't true, or at least it is not the whole truth. You see, I took that verse out of its context. As a wise theologian once said, "A text without a context is a pretext."

📖 Look again at James 4:6–10. What ideas come before and after the call to resist?

_____

_____

_____

James precedes the admonition to resist the devil with another command: *"Submit therefore to God,"* and he follows it with the charge to *"draw near to God."* While it is true that all I have to do is resist, James makes it clear that I have to walk with God in order to be able to resist. If I focus only on resisting the devil, I am in danger of trying to accomplish that in my own strength. What I need to recognize is that when I submit to God and when I draw near to God, I am *also* resisting the devil.

But when we resist the devil, what exactly are we resisting? What is he trying to do? According to Scripture, all of Satan's schemes have one objective: to lead us astray *"from the simplicity and purity of devotion to Christ"* (2 Corinthians 11:3). All of Satan's schemes are aimed at steering me away from my walk with Christ. When I submit to the Lord, when I draw near to Him, I *am* resisting the devil. I am doing the opposite of what he wants. "But wait," some will say, "none of us is perfect. Does that mean that if I stop submitting to the Lord I will be overcome by the devil?" Notice what else James says in verse 8: *"Cleanse your hands, you sinners; and purify your hearts, you double-minded."* You see, James recognizes that, as he put it earlier in his book, *"We all stumble in many ways"* (James 3:2). Another facet of resisting the devil is dealing with it when I commit sin. Notice, I said *when,* because we all sin. James says we are to "cleanse our hands" (this means cleaning up our actions through confession and repentance) and "purify our hearts" (this means dealing with attitudes the same way). If I keep short accounts with God about my sin, and keep coming back to a position of surrender, I will experience victory in spiritual battle.

In Ephesians Paul speaks of the need to *"stand firm against the schemes of the devil."* It sounds a lot like the idea of resisting, doesn't it? If fact, the word translated "stand" here is *histemi.* The only difference is that instead of using the prefix *anti* (meaning "against"), Paul uses *pros.* Together with *histemi* it means "to stand before" or "to stand in the face of." Both convey the intention of standing. According to James, I stand against the devil by standing with and submitting to God. What does Paul say? He says, *"Put on the full armor of God, that you may be able to stand firm against [in the face of] the schemes of the devil."* He precedes this statement with the call to *"be strong in the Lord, and in the strength of His might."* I can't stand before the schemes of the devil in my own strength. I can only stand before him in the strength of the Lord. I only have access to the *"strength of His might"* as I am submitted

> **All of Satan's schemes have one objective: to lead us astray from the "simplicity and purity of devotion to Christ."**
>
> **2 Corinthians 11:3**

to Him without any unconfessed sin in my life. To submit to the Lord and to confess my sins is to put on the full armor of God. When I yield my life to the Lord's control, I have *"put on the Lord Jesus"* (Romans 13:14). When I put on the Lord Jesus I have the armor, because He is my armor.

HELP IN STANDING FIRM

When it comes to physically standing, most of us haven't really had to think about it since we were toddlers; we just do it. The practice requires little attention or intentionality. The reason is simple. It is not an activity that is normally opposed. However, if you were a sumo wrestler or an offensive lineman on a football team, it would be a different story. If someone were trying to knock you over, everything would change. You would be alert. You would brace yourself for contact from the opponent. You would attempt to counter his attack. Realize this important fact: if you want to keep standing spiritually, you must have the same approach.

This word *histemi* is repeated four times in Ephesians 6:10–18. Three of these are translated "stand." The fourth usage is translated "resist." The most important thing in spiritual warfare is to remain standing. I don't need to attack the devil; I just need to not allow him to keep me from standing in Christ. If you want a better understanding of what it means to "stand," then you'll want to examine how *histemi* is used elsewhere in the New Testament. That is what we will focus on, and today we will look at its usage by the apostle Paul.

📖 Reflect on Romans 5:1–2. What does this passage tell us about standing?

_____

_____

_____

Our word *histemi* shows up in the second verse. Interestingly, it is associated here with grace. It is important to recognize the role that grace plays in enabling us to remain standing. We stand by God's grace, not just by our efforts and striving. We entered this grace by faith (placing our trust in the Lord), and we stand in it by faith as well.

 Paul uses *histemi* again in Romans 14:4. What speaks to you from this usage?

_____

_____

_____

> **"Therefore let him who thinks he stands take heed that he does not fall."**
>
> **1 Corinthians 10:12**

To these Roman believers, Paul gives a sense of purpose in standing. We stand to our master and to His pleasure. What a comfort it is to know that the Lord is able to make us stand! Proverbs 24:16 states that *"a righteous man falls seven times, and rises again."* When we do stumble, the Lord assists us in getting back up. Again we see that our ability to stand is from Him.

Histemi also occurs in 1 Corinthians 10:12. What new information do you glean there?

_____

_____

This is an interesting exhortation. It raises the possibility that we can think we are standing securely when we aren't. Of course, the admonition emphasizes our need to be alert. Following this verse, Paul immediately moves to speaking of temptation. The take-home point is this: One of the safest ways to guard against falling is being willing to admit that you can. We stand securely as we recognize temptation when it comes our way and choose, through the power of the Spirit, to say no to it.

STANDING FIRM IN THE FAITH

Have you ever lost your footing and injured yourself? Walking on wet or icy ground can be treacherous and makes it much easier to slip. On a college ski excursion, I sprained my ankle rather badly. I'm a pretty adventurous person—not one to play it safe. I had "hot-dogged" it all over the slopes the whole day without a single spill or injury. At closing time I turned in my rented equipment and met up with my group. As I walked across the parking lot, I was mentally congratulating myself on how well I had skied. I wasn't, however, paying close attention to where I was walking. An unnoticed patch of ice gave me a valuable, albeit somewhat painful, lesson in firm footing. As I limped back to the car, assisted by my friends, a passerby inquired, "Tough day on the slopes?" I didn't have the heart to tell him the real story.

When you walk on unstable terrain, you have to take care to pick secure places for your footing. The same is true spiritually. We have talked a lot about *how* we stand. A good question to ask at this point is, "*Where* do we stand?"

📖 The word *histemi* shows up again in 2 Corinthians 1:24. What does this passage teach about *where* we stand?

_____

_____

_____

We stand "in our faith." Actually, this verse addresses both the "where" and the "how" of our standing. You see, in the original Greek manuscript there is no personal pronoun employed with the word faith. Instead, there is something called the "definite article." The definite article makes a word specific. In the English language we express this sense of definiteness by prefacing an expression with "the" – such as "*the* word." We speak of something generally by saying "*a* word." Most of the time, when faith is referenced with this definite article, it isn't talking about faith in the sense of our trust in God. Instead, it means THE faith—the whole of Christian teaching and belief. "The faith" speaks to the Christian life rightly lived. **Trust** is important in securing our spiritual victory, but the call to stand firm in the faith reveals how essential **truth** is as well.

Word Study
BIBLE STUDY TOOL BOX

When a Greek word appears with the definite article, we refer to it as "articular." If the remark has no article, it is called "anarthrous." If you aren't able to read Greek but would like to be able to distinguish such points as the definite article, the meaning of the Greek word, or the tense, voice, and mood of verbs, let me recommend two excellent tools. *The Key Word Study Bible* makes Greek background accessible for key terms. *The Complete Word Study New Testament* includes such information for every single word in the New Testament. Both are products from AMG Publishers and are available from your local Christian bookstore.

How do we stand firm in the Christian faith? Obviously we need to know what we believe. Developing our doctrine produces stability in our walk. Participating in this study is a step in that direction. As you think rightly and think biblically, you become more stable and less easily led astray by Satan's lies.

📖 Returning to one of our major passages on warfare, what do you see in 1 Peter 5:9 that supports this idea of standing in the faith?

_____

_____

_____

When the apostle Peter speaks of "faith" here, he also employs the definite article. Although the New American Standard version translates it "your" faith, there is no personal pronoun in the Greek text, although there could be. To me it makes more sense to translate this phrase "firm in THE faith." You see, rightly living the Christian life is how I stand, and the true Christian faith is where I stand. It I want to be able to resist the adversary, I need to stand on the solid ground of Scripture. As we saw last week, the *"sword of the Spirit"* is identified here as *"the word of* God," but the Greek term translated *"word"* is not the one typically used. Normally the Greek expression would be *logos* (from which we get our term "logic"). When applied to the Bible, it means the Bible as a whole. Here however, the term used is not speaking of the Bible as a whole (if it were, Paul would have used the Greek word *logos* instead of *rhema*). It means spoken word. The weapon Paul references here isn't the Bible as a whole. Instead, my sword in battle is the specific Scriptures the Spirit helps me apply to my circumstance.

📖 Examine Ephesians 6:16 and record what you observe that supports this important role of right belief in our victory.

_____

_____

_____

In this verse we again see the word "faith" appearing with the definite article. A literal translation would be "the shield of the faith" (Christian doctrine).

Remember, we were tracing the word "stand" (*histemi*) through the New Testament.

📖 How does Peter's use of the word "stand" in 1 Peter 5:12 increase your understanding of the concept.

_____

_____

_____

You should recall that this verse immediately follows Peter's words about spiritual warfare. He has just admonishing believers to resist the devil by standing firm in the faith. In verse 12 he says, *"I have written to you briefly, exhorting and testifying that this is the true grace of God. Stand firm in it!"* There is no more important action in the Christian life than to "stand." Because of this, our enemy's greates aim is to knock us off our feet.

Did You Know?
WORDS IN ITALICS

The New American Standard translation of 1 Peter 5:9 places the word *"your"* in italics. In this version (and most others), when the translators do this they are communicating that the word doesn't actually appear in the ancient text but is merely suggested. Such added words are not heretical, but are a more subjective interpretation.

As we look at these three passages on spiritual warfare, it is crucial to recognize that Peter, James, and Paul are not saying three different things. As we study the texts, it becomes obvious that they are really saying the same thing three different ways. Each places the emphasis on differing points, but that is because of the specific needs of each audience. The main point in each passage is "standing firm in the faith" to resist the devil. Peter emphasizes that we are to humbly cast upon the Lord our cares which come from our sufferings. James stresses dealing with the sin which creeps into our lives. Paul calls attention to three weapons to be used in our battle:

The shield of [THE] faith, which refers to our pursuit of the faith.

The sword of the Spirit, which refers to a lifestyle of immersing ourselves in the Word of God so that we may draw upon it by the Spirit in our time of need.

Spirit-praying, not as a ritual or through the use of mystic formulas, but our spirit connecting with His Spirit about everything.

The bottom line in spiritual warfare is maintaining a healthy walk with Christ. That is our security. If we **trust** the Lord and stand in **truth**, we always have firm footing in our faith.

HOW TO REMAIN STANDING

You have probably heard and even used the phrase, "the last man standing." No one really knows for sure where the expression comes from, but one of the most famous historical examples of the concept is attributed to a man we know as Custer. Five companies of the 7th U. S. Cavalry, under the command of Major General George Armstrong Custer, died with their leader on June 25, 1876, near the Little Bighorn River in what is now Montana. Although another part of the regiment who had been pinned down a few miles away was eventually rescued, no one from Custer's command survived the battle. In the 1941 movie *They Died With Their Boots On,* the swashbuckling Custer is pictured as a gallant hero who fights to the bitter end against overwhelming odds. This "last man standing" is portrayed running out of bullets and then standing beside the American flag as Chief Crazy Horse takes his life. As usual, Hollywood glamorized the story with no small amount of revisionist history. Today, Custer is more commonly reviled than revered. He is accused of brutally murdering unarmed Native American women and children and being an inept commander whose blunders led to the slaughter of his men.

Was Custer really the last man standing at Little Bighorn? Since no white man survived the skirmish, it is a pretty hard story to validate. Most now believe that his ill-fated attack was driven by personal vanity and an arrogant pursuit of glory. As to his death, there were surviving eyewitnesses from among the Native Americans who fought in the conflict. David Humphreys Miller authored an account of the battle, including Custer's death, based on interviews conducted with 71 Indian survivors of the Custer clash in their native language.[1] Weaving their testimony together, he speculates that Custer was the first casualty from among his men. He was shot in the chest as he led his men across the river in the first engagement with the Cheyenne. His men pulled him to safety on the hill where his body was eventually found. The only other wound on his body was a bullet hole in his left temple that many believe was self-inflicted.

In the context of spiritual war, being the last man standing is not the result of bravery and braggadocio, but of humility and dependence on God. If we want to keep standing, we would do well to heed Paul's advice to the Corinthians: *"Let him who thinks he stands take heed that he does not fall"* (1 Corinthians 10:12).

📖 How, according to 1 Corinthians 16:13-14, are we to "stand" in the faith?

_____

_____

_____

First Corinthians 16:13–14 issues five challenges, each relating to how the believer is to stand in the faith. In the Greek text, each appears in the "imperative mood," meaning they are commands, not suggestions. He charges:

> *Be on the alert*
> *Stand firm in the faith*
> *Act like men (grown-ups, not children)*
> *Be strong*
> *Let all that you do be done in love*

In these five exhortations we find essentials for spiritual warfare. The battle really is about Satan trying to tear down our walk with Christ. These five admonitions serve to protect that walk. Let's look at these truths.

First, we are exhorted to *"be on the alert."* This same idea can be found in Peter's treatise on warfare (1 Peter 5:8) and in Paul's as well (Ephesians 6:18). We need to have an awareness of the battle. We must accept that Satan will be persistent in his efforts to tempt us and lure us away from the faith. One of the surest ways to fall is to think that we would never fall. There is security in admitting how easily we could stumble, for this fuels alertness.

📖 What, according to 2 Corinthians 2:11, is one of the ways Satan can trip us up?

_____

_____

_____

In 2 Corinthians chapter 2 Paul is speaking of forgiveness and the danger of withholding it. In verse 11 he identifies why forgiveness is so important. We must forgive *"so that no advantage would be taken of us by Satan,* **for we are not ignorant of his schemes"** (emphasis mine). One of those schemes is to tempt us to hold on to grudges and grievances. If Satan is successful at that, he has an advantage. He can distract us from the things we ought to be about, and he can rob us of our joy.

We need be aware of Satan's schemes, not just generally, but specifically. We need to look honestly at our lives and recognize where he usually strikes us personally. If anger or bitterness or unforgiveness is a frequent place of failure, we should be especially vigilant in these areas.

Word Study
VERBS

Greek grammatical structure presents main verbs that represent the central action, as well as modifying verbs (participles and infinitives) that lend support to these main verbs. Central verbs are always accompanied by a mood. Greek verb moods are:

Imperative: commands

Indicative: statements of fact

Subjunctive: mood of uncertainty (usually conditional)

Optative: mood of wish or desire

📖 Look at Matthew 24:24 and identify what danger this verse alerts us to.

_____

_____

_____

In addition to temptation, we also need to be on the alert for false teaching. In Matthew 24:24 Jesus warns that in the end times, *"False Christs and false prophets will arise and will show great signs and wonders, so as to mislead, if possible, even the elect."* We need to be alert against false teaching. Perhaps no verse in the New Testament is more sobering than 1 Timothy 4:1 which says: *"But the Spirit explicitly says that in later times some will fall away from the faith, paying attention to deceitful spirits and doctrines of demons."*

As our Lord's return draws near, more and more belief systems of demonic origin will surface in society. We must be on the alert for all false teaching—especially wrong teaching about Satan and warfare. Think about it. If deception is one of his favorite tricks, rest assured he would like nothing more than to deceive us in our view of him.

The second exhortation is to *"stand firm in the faith."* As we have already discussed, the Christian life rightly lived is crucial to spiritual stability. How do we stand firm in the faith? James says, *"Draw near to the Lord...cleanse your hands...and purify your hearts."* I must stay in God's word, and I must maintain my fellowship with Him. In Galatians 5:16 Paul puts it simply, *"Walk by the Spirit, and you will not carry out the desire of the flesh."*

Third is the admonition to *"act like men."* This does not mean that only men can walk with Christ. To paraphrase, Paul is saying,, "Act like grown-ups, not like kids." We must pursue maturity. The Corinthian church got into trouble because, though they had known Christ for a long time, they hadn't progressed very far spiritually. They were still spiritual *"infants"* (see 1 Corinthians 3:1). They hadn't made it out of the nursery. If we want to fully experience the victory that is ours in Christ, we must pursue maturity. I like the way Paul expresses this idea in Ephesians 4:14–15: *"We are no longer to be children, tossed here and there by waves, and carried about by every wind of doctrine...but speaking the truth in love, we are to grow up in all aspects into Him who is the head."*

The fourth call to Corinth, and to us, is to *"be strong."* Paul doesn't go into the same level of detail here, but the idea is the same one he expresses in Ephesians 6:10. We are to *"be strong in the Lord and in the strength of His might."* We are to be strong, but not in our strength. If our trust is in self, we will try to live out our Christian commitment in our own strength. If we recognize how much we need the Lord's aid to battle the adversary, and we surrender, yielding each area to Christ, He becomes the source of our strength.

Paul concludes his spiritual challenges with a final charge to *"let all that you do be done in love."* The love spoken of here is *agape*, God's unconditional love. God doesn't merely desire that we do the right thing. He also wants our actions accomplished from a right attitude. The Corinthian church was stained with selfish behavior, and thus was being torn apart at the seams. Love is the bond of God's body.

Word Study
SCHEMES

There are two main Greek words translated "scheme" in the New Testament: *methodia* and *noema*. The first term connotes working methodically in step-by-step fashion. The second word signifies a concept of the mind, or a device. The former refers to implementation, while the latter refers to strategy. It is this second word that is translated "schemes" in 2 Corinthians 2:11.

"Stand firm in the faith."

> **"Be angry, and yet do not sin; do not let the sun go down on your anger, and do not give the devil an opportunity."**
>
> **Ephesians 4:26–27**

📖 What trap of the enemy does Ephesians 4:26–27 reveal?

_____

_____

_____

Paul instructs, *"Be angry, and yet do not sin; do not let the sun go down on your anger, and* **do not give the devil an opportunity"** (emphasis mine). The Bible doesn't say that all anger is sin. But anger turns to sin when it is held in our hearts and not confronted. When we are angry with our brother and we do not express love by working through it, we give the devil opportunity to attack us in our relationships. He delights to divide. It is imperative we never lose sight of love, for *"love covers a multitude of sins"* (1 Peter 4:8).

Paul's five commands to the Corinthians occur at the end of that book. He wants them to be a final thought. They make an appropriate end to our look at the believer's offense: *"Be on the alert, stand firm in the faith, act like men, be strong. Let all that you do be done in love."* If we live out those exhortations, our worries with the devil will be lessened.

FOR ME TO FOLLOW GOD

Have you ever played the game "King of the Hill"? I spent many hours with my friends in this adolescent diversion. The hill varied from a fencepost to a pile of dirt. One person would claim the high ground, and then it would become the objective of everyone else to pull him off of his perch. It seemed that no one remained "king" for long when we were kids, because the king was always outnumbered. Fortunately, the odds are more in our favor in the spiritual version of this game. We don't have to hold the high ground alone, and the Lord's army is larger than Lucifer's. The aim is still the same though—Satan wants to drag us down. Our objective is to resist him and to keep standing.

 As you meditate on the admonition to *"stand firm"* against the schemes of the devil, consider which schemes he seems to frequently employ against you?

_____

_____

_____

_____

In James 4:7–8, two measures are encouraged: submission to God and drawing near to God. Both are crucial in spiritual warfare. At the present time, are you walking in submission to God? You needn't wonder. God lives in you in the person of the Holy Spirit. If you want to know if He is in control, all you have to do is ask. David prayed in Psalm 139:23–24, *"Search me, O God, and know my heart; Try me and know my anxious thoughts; And see if there be any hurtful way in me, And lead me in the everlasting way."* Why not make this your prayer, inviting the Lord to reveal any weaknesses in your submission to Him.

The second action James calls for is to *"draw near"* to God. Obviously, since James is writing to believers, he doesn't mean the initial drawing near to God that occurs at salvation. Instead, it would seem he is advocating the habit of drawing near to God. On the scale below, circle the number of days in the past week that you drew near to the Lord through prayer and Scripture meditation. Then place a square around the figure that you feel represents the number of days in the average week that you spend time with the Lord.

0   1   2   3   4   5   6   7

APPLY   If you are going to stand your ground in this spiritual struggle, it will not be accomplished in your own strength. What weaker areas of your walk with Christ do you feel make you vulnerable to attack?

_____

_____

_____

Paul spoke of taking up *"the shield of faith"* in Ephesians 6:16, the shield of THE faith—our doctrine. He tells us to take up *"the sword of the Spirit,"* the Scriptures the Holy Spirit brings to mind in our time of need. Regular time in God's Word is the fuel that energizes both of these actions. When Jesus encountered the devil in the wilderness (Matthew 4), He countered each of Satan's three temptations by responding with Scripture.

APPLY   Completing this Bible study is a step in the right direction, but what do you plan to do to continue growing in God's Word once this study is done?

_____

_____

_____

_____

One of the founders of the Southern Baptist Convention, John Broadus, is considered by many to be the father of modern preaching. His text, *On the Preparation and Delivery of a Sermon*, was an instant classic and helped to shape preaching values for subsequent generations of pastors. In a seminary class he taught just days before his death, he addressed a gathering of students and taught them about Apollos. Referencing the description Luke gives of Apollos in Acts 18:24, Dr. Broadus exhorted his students that the need of the hour was saints *"mighty in the Scriptures."* He repeated the charge several times. What is needed today in the raging spiritual war is that all of us be *"mighty in the Scriptures."* That is the surest safeguard against the lies and deceit of the enemy.

Which of the following do you believe God is calling you to do in order to arm yourself for spiritual warfare:

____ Read through the entire Bible over the course of the next year
____ Enroll in a weekly Bible study class for encouragement and accountability
____ Purchase Bible study tools and seek to become a more diligent student of the Word
____ Regularly take notes on sermons and Scripture lessons
____ Other:_____

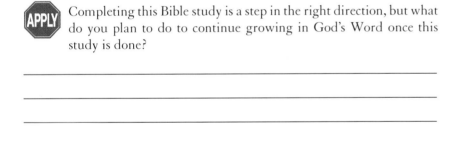

If you are going to stand your ground in this spiritual struggle, it will not be accomplished in your own strength.

In Day Four, we considered two ways that the devil could gain an advantage over us. Both of these involved dangers to our relationships with fellow Christians. The first was an unwillingness to forgive others (2 Corinthians 2:10–11), and the second was unresolved anger (Ephesians 4:26–27).

APPLY Are there any brothers or sisters in Christ whom you have not forgiven for wrongs they have committed?

_____

_____

_____

_____

Have you allowed "the sun to go down" on any recent issues of anger without resolving them?

_____

_____

_____

_____

Spiritual warfare is not mystical dealings with spirit beings. It is intensely practical. True warfare means protecting my walk from Satan's strategies, and if I stumble, quickly returning to a position of "standing firm." In your closing prayer, purpose in your heart to deal with any unresolved relationship issues so that no advantage can be taken of you by the devil.

_____

_____

_____

_____

_____

_____

_____

_____

_____

_____

Works Cited

1. David Humphreys Miller, *Custer's Fall* (New York: Duell, Sloan and Pearce,1957).

2. "John A. Broadus," *The Reformed Reader,* http://www.reformedreader.org/rbb/broadus/biography.htm.

Notes

Notes

7

Questioning What Is Questionable in Warfare Practices

The classical Greek philosopher Socrates is considered one of the fathers of Western ethics and thinking. What we know of him doesn't come from his books, since he wrote none. He believed arguing and debating a subject was superior to a written monologue. Instead, the ideas of Socrates have lived on in the writings of his pupils. His most famous student, Plato, once called him "the wisest and justest and best of all men I have ever known."[1] The writings of Plato, Xenophon, and others introduced the world to what has become known as the "Socratic Method" of instruction. Although the Oracle of Delphi pronounced him the wisest man in Greece, Socrates didn't view himself that way. Though his contemporaries often claimed to know more than they did, he seemed to grasp the limited scope of his own knowledge. His humble and self-effacing approach to instruction was to answer a question with another question, forcing his pupil to think. Often, he claimed not to know the answers of the questions he asked, because Socrates saw asking questions as the key to learning. When teachers ask questions that encourage their students to process the many sides of an issue and draw conclusions, they are using this "Socratic Method."

This study in spiritual warfare seeks to arm you, the believer, with practical answers grounded in truth to your questions on dealing with the devil. At this point, you probably still have questions. This week's ambition is to help you examine for yourself

> *The key to good Bible study is asking good questions.*

the questionable and controversial aspects of our topic and the Scriptures that are employed in defense of them. You will be called to ask questions of each practice and take personal ownership of your answers. Central to good Bible study is asking good questions. The key is to do your homework (figuratively and literally). None of us aims to draw conclusions without all the facts. Yet sometimes we do. What we believe and what we practice are often shaped by something other than our own diligent study. As we tackle some sticky questions this week, bring a teachable, inquisitive attitude. If not all of your questions get answered, at least you will move to a deeper understanding of what you can confidently accept as Biblical and where caution is warranted.

We will start each day's discussion by identifying the verses people use in support of problematic activities. My desire is not to throw stones at those with differing views, but to honestly give a defense for what I believe and to help you decide for yourself. Where the Scriptures are clear, I will point that out. If a practice stems from unclear teaching, I will point you to the emphasis of God's Word as a whole. Most importantly, where I just don't know, I'll be honest and say that. My goal is to help those who are confused sort through their bewilderments in a way that honors the Lord and His Word. Let me warn you up front: You may find that some of your beliefs about spiritual warfare and the demonic are challenged. I am not the authority here—God's word is. I only ask that you enter this lesson with a heart teachable to what the Bible has to say and allow it be your final authority. Let's begin by asking some questions!

DELIVERANCE MINISTRY AND THE CHRISTIAN

Can a Christian be demon-possessed? We know from Scriptural history that some people have been overcome and inhabited by an evil spirit. That much is clear. It is a special concern for us to know the powers and limits of Satan's minions in their dealings with those who belong to Christ. As a young Christian, I sought counsel along with a girl I was dating at the time. I didn't really know the pastor we went to, but he had been recommended highly by a friend. The girl and I had been having conflict, but we weren't ready to give up on the relationship. We wanted to try to work through our difficulties in a way that would honor the Lord. After only a couple of questions, the pastor informed us he had identified the root problem. We needed deliverance. Our difficulties were symptoms of a demon that needed to be cast out. He considered himself somewhat of an expert at this and was ready to go to work. The first step, he said, was to determine the "window" or means by which the demon had entered. He gave us both a printout that listed hundreds of different sins. Our mission, should we choose to accept it, was to review it prayerfully and mark every sin we had ever committed. We did work through our conflict, but we didn't go back for the second appointment with the pastor. Through prayer, searching the Scriptures, and godly counsel from spiritual mentors who knew us, we eventually recognized that the root of the conflict wasn't a demon—it was our own flesh. God used the conflict to show us areas in each of our lives He wanted to work in.

I am sure the pastor who counseled us had the best of intentions, but he didn't know us and didn't take the time to know our situation. I now realize that his theology had conditioned him to interpret everything negative as demon-induced. He believed that Christians could be possessed by a demon, and when that happened they needed someone like him to exorcise the offending spirit. We know from Scripture that demons can sometimes inhabit people. Are Christians vulnerable to this danger? If so, how is the problem solved? The answer to this question strikes at the very core of how we deal with sin and walk with God.

This particular question can be broken down into several related queries. Demons can possess humans, but do Christians have any added defense? If we can't be possessed (owned), can we be "oppressed?" What is the difference between the two? If a Christian can be demon-possessed or oppressed, how is the evil spirit to be removed? Finally, if demons are to blame for the sin issues in our lives instead of our flesh, does this mean we are not responsible for our actions? As you can see, this really isn't just one question.

In addition to Gospel accounts that speak of demon possession generically, one passage proponents of "deliverance ministry" use in support of the idea is Ephesians 4:26–27. Look at these verses in their context.

APPLY What do you think it means to *"give the devil an opportunity"*?

_____

_____

_____

What solution does this passage offer?

_____

_____

_____

Clearly the idea of unresolved anger is linked with giving the devil *"an opportunity."* The KJV translates opportunity as *"give place,"* and in the NIV it is rendered *"foothold."* Some take this to mean a demonic habitation in the life of a believer. The Greek word (*topos*) can mean a literal place of occupation or can be used metaphorically of an occasion or opportunity (see Acts 25:16). If one takes this to mean a demonic possession, why does Paul say *"give the devil an opportunity"* instead of "give a demon an opportunity?" Even if this means a literal place of occupation, the context suggests this place is in a believer's relationship with another, not in a believer himself. I would not consider this a very strong argument for the idea that a Christian can have a demon. Particularly problematic is that all the solutions Paul offers revolve around repentance, not deliverance. He charges believers to *"put away"* anger, along with any accompanying bitterness, wrath, and malice (v. 31), and exhorts forgiveness (v. 32). My interpretation of this verse is, "Don't give Satan the opportunity to hinder God's work in your life and relationships by drawing you away from being yielded to the Spirit."

Another text cited as proof for the possibility of Christians having a demon is Matthew 16:23. Read this verse and those immediately around it and reflect on the questions that follow.

What in this passage supports the idea that Peter is inhabited by Satan?

_____

_____

Can a Christian be demon-possessed? The answers to this question strikes at the very core of how we deal with sin and walk with God.

"Be angry, and yet do not sin; do not let the sun go down on your anger, and do not give the devil an opportunity."

Ephesians 4:26–27

Is Peter a Christian at this point in the same way you and I are?

_____

_____

_____

_____

Does Jesus cast out the offensive spirit or apply any specific solution?

_____

_____

_____

Some have suggested Peter was possessed by Satan when he was rebuked here by Christ. Yet Peter has just uttered the great confession, *"You are the Christ, the Son of the Living God"* (Matthew 16:16). In verse 17 Jesus pronounced him blessed and made clear that the Heavenly Father had revealed this to him. Though Peter was a follower of Christ at this point, this occurred before Pentecost, when believers were indwelt by the Spirit (John 7:39; Acts 2). Jesus didn't say Peter was possessed. Instead His rebuke placed the blame on Peter's thinking. My flesh can align itself with Satan's will and wishes instead of God's. We see a similar confrontation in Luke 9:54–55 when the disciples wanted to call down fire from heaven on an inhospitable village. Jesus said, *"You do not know what kind of spirit you are of."* This is not the same as demon-possession, in which an individual is forced to act against his own will. Instead, these accounts show that any of us can exercise our wills to pursue the direction of the devil instead of following the Lord. When he said Christ shouldn't be killed, Peter's mind was focused on what his flesh desired, and he missed God's will. Jesus didn't cast Satan out of Peter. Instead, He charged all the disciples to deny self, take up their own crosses, and follow Him. Let me draw your attention to an additional point: In Matthew 16:18 Jesus says that upon Peter's revelation that He [Jesus] is the Christ, the church would be built, *"and the gates of Hades will not overpower it."*

A third passage used by some to argue that Christians can be demon-possessed or oppressed is found in 2 Corinthians 12:7–10. Examine this passage and respond to the listed inquiries.

Where was Paul's thorn and where did it come from?

_____

_____

_____

_____

How was he delivered from this affliction?

_____

_____

_____

_____

Some scholars believe Paul's problem was a physical disease such as eye trouble. Others have suggested it was a battle with an area of recurring sin

> "When he said Christ shouldn't be killed, Peter's mind was focused on what his flesh desired, and he missed God's will."

such as pride. Paul does not identify what his "thorn" was. However, he does tell us where it resided—"*in the flesh.*" It does seem to be internal. Further, it is called a *"messenger"* (literally "angel") of Satan. One can understand why some would understand this as inhabitation by a demon. Certainly Paul is a Christian, indwelt by the Holy Spirit. Does this defend the deliverance concept? If so, then both Paul's response to this infirmity and the ultimate outcome are problematic. Paul does not rebuke his thorn or command it to leave in Jesus' name. Instead he repeatedly, but unsuccessfully, asks God to remove it. Did the effort fail because of a lack of faith or assistance? On this point the text is clear. God was unwilling to remove the thorn. Instead, He wanted Paul to lean on His sufficient grace. At this, Paul considered the matter closed. He boasted of his problem and took ownership of it. He identified it as *"my weaknesses."*

I have been offered the incident of Ananias and Saphira from Acts 5 as Biblical proof a Christian could have a demon. Peter does inquire of Ananias, *"Why has Satan filled your heart"* (Acts 5:3). Once again, however, the outcome refutes rather than affirms deliverance ministry. Instead of the demon being cast out, Ananias is struck dead. I'm not sure many want to sign up for this kind of deliverance. Some have employed Luke 13:11–16 to support the premise that demons can inhabit Christians. The passage states clearly that the woman *"had a sickness caused by a spirit."* Jesus stated that Satan had *"bound"* her for 18 years and He released her from bondage. Was she a Christian? Jesus identifies her as *"a daughter of Abraham"* (Luke 13:16). Again, however, this occurs before Pentecost. I should also mention King Saul. Once he was rejected as king, the Spirit of God left him and an *"evil spirit from the Lord"* began to torment him (1 Samuel 16:14–23). It is noteworthy that the Spirit of the Lord had to leave for the evil spirit to come. Of course, in this sense the Old Testament believer is different than his New Testament counterpart. Before Pentecost, the Holy Spirit temporarily indwelt only certain believers for special tasks. Since Pentecost, believers are permanently indwelt by the Spirit at salvation and He never leaves (Hebrews 13:5).

Can a Christian be possessed? It is a sensitive question, and we can only draw inferences from what Scripture does say. I believe the weight of Scripture leans to a "no" answer. There is no clear biblical example of any New Testament Christian being possessed. In the accounts used in support of this idea, not one of the individuals is clearly demon-possessed. More problematic is that in none of these cases is the purported demon cast out. Further, a demon inhabiting a Christian seems incompatible with the Holy Spirit permanently residing in the believer. How could a demon possess what already belongs to God? All biblical instances of casting out demons are in the context of evangelizing unbelievers. The notion of Christians being possessed by demons is in direct conflict with a clear statement of Scripture: *"We know that no one who is born of God sins;* ["sins" is in the present tense meaning "sins continuously and habitually"] *but He who was born of God* [Jesus] *keeps him* [the believer] *and the evil one* **does not touch him"** (1 John 5:18, emphasis mine). *"Touch"* here doesn't mean a light brush. It is a stronger word meaning "to manipulate." I believe Christians can encounter the demonic, but Christ won't allow us to be manipulated or controlled. *"Greater is He who is in you than he who is in the world"* (1 John 4:4).

"We know that no one who is born of God sins; but He who was born of God keeps him, and the evil one does not touch him."
- 1 John 5:18

STRONGHOLDS, FORTRESSES, AND TAKING THOUGHTS CAPTIVE

A compelling scene in Tolkien's fictional epic *The Lord of the Rings* is the battle at Helm's Deep. Helm's Deep, a fortress positioned against steep mountain walls, had been built by the kings of Gondor as a safe haven for their people. It was said that Helm's Deep would never fall while men defended it. No enemy had ever breached the fortress' "Deeping Wall" or set foot inside. That changes in the battle between Rohan and the wizard Saruman's army. Amid much bloodshed and with the aid of sorcery, this evil army breaks through the barricade. The story's heroes are forced to find final refuge in a cave. After deliberation, it is deemed better to die a noble death than to surrender. They charge forth from the cave to face certain destruction and are surprised by their friend Gandalf and reinforcements. The tide of the battle turns in their favor. This dramatic encounter vividly captures all of the imagery we associate with great fortresses and battles between good and evil.

For many, this is our idea of a fortress, and the thought of Satan setting up a fortress or stronghold in our lives is indeed fearful. Is it possible? David called God his *"stronghold"* in 2 Samuel 22:3. However, in spiritual warfare discussions the term is used to refer to a beachhead of Satan in a believer's life. It is alleged by some that delivering a Christian requires tearing down strongholds. What are these strongholds and how are they torn down? One deliverance website defines a "stronghold" this way:

> A stronghold is a faulty thinking pattern based on lies and deception. Deception is one of the primary weapons of the devil, because it is the building blocks for a stronghold. What strongholds can do is cause us to think in ways which block us from God's best. For example, if you think you have to confess all your sins to everybody you've ever wronged, you'll feel just awful and guilty until you do all that, and even then, you'll probably feel guilty, because you probably forgot many people that you didn't confess your sins to. All unnecessary, and a waste of time, all because you were deceived and thought that you had to do something that you really didn't have to do.[2]

The writer believes a stronghold to be an area of a believer's life where the Devil gains entry by deceiving their thinking. The author goes on to identify some common strongholds and provides instructions on how we should begin to tear them down. For example, he writes, "If you feel God is distant and cold, or question if God loves you, then you need to get this stronghold torn down." This deliverance website claims "strongholds are torn down as we meditate on God's Word, which is truth!" I certainly agree with the need for us to be in the Scriptures. I whole-heartedly join hands with this brother in encouraging you to study your Bible and meditate on the truths found there. But the question still remains: What is a stronghold? Is it an area where Satan has freedom to operate? Even if I cannot be possessed, could a portion of my mind be inhabited by the enemy? That is the issue we tackle today.

📖 Read 2 Corinthians 10:1–6.

With whom or against what is Paul waging war?

_____

_____

_____

APPLY What do you see in these verses that could lead one to believe Satan can establish a fortress or stronghold in a believer's mind?

_____

_____

_____

_____

"For though we walk in the flesh, we do not war according to the flesh."

2 Corinthians 10:3

The terminology used makes it plain that this passage is about spiritual warfare. Paul talks of destroying *"fortresses ["strongholds" in the KJV] . . . speculations and every lofty thing raised up against the knowledge of God."* It is crucial to identify the opponent in the battle. In verse 2 Paul speaks of being *"courageous against some."* A central theme in 2 Corinthians is the apostle's concern over false teachers who had crept into the church, and apparently he has them in mind. It is safe to associate the *"weapons"* of his warfare with the sword of the spirit and shield of faith from Ephesians 6. Paul says *"We are taking every thought captive to the obedience of Christ."* Does this mean Satan can put thoughts in our minds? Can he read our minds and know what we are thinking? Examine the text closely. Paul has specific people in mind here. While they may be tools of Satan, the false teachers are neither the devil nor demons. They are human agents doing harm in the church. We should next ask, Where are these strongholds Paul speaks of? Are they in the mind of an individual or in the church as a whole?

📖 Look up the word *"thought"* from verse 5 in a Greek dictionary (it is the Greek word *noema*), or consult an English dictionary and write down what you learn.

_____

_____

_____

The *Random House Unabridged Dictionary* (2006) tells us the word "thought" can mean "a single act or product of thinking" or it can mean "the product of mental activity." The Greek word *noema* means "a thought, a concept of the mind," but can also mean "a device, a contrivance." At its core, *noema* simply means "the results of the mind"—all a person's thinking, or just one part. The root word (*nous*) means "mind." The suffix *-ma* adds the idea of results. The word *noema* sometimes refers to a way of thinking or a philosophy held by many. How do we distinguish which meaning to apply? The same way we do when an English word has several possible meanings—we determine which fits the context of the conversation. What makes this particular passage difficult is that the context is a little vague. We normally assume it is speaking of a single thought in an individual's head, but that is shaped more by what we take into the text than what can be drawn out of it. When I face this type of uncertainty with the meaning of a word, I study how the word is used elsewhere in the Bible.

We must learn to recognize the lies of the enemy that we have believed, and replace them with the truth of God's Word.

In 2 Corinthians 2:11 Paul uses *noema* in speaking of Satan. He writes, *"For we are not ignorant of his schemes."* In this instance the word seems to refer to strategies, not just individual thoughts. In 2 Corinthians 3:14, 4:4 and 11:3, and in Philippians 4:7, *noema* is translated "minds." Paul employs the term to speak of the whole of a person's thinking. We've now looked at every use of *noema* in the New Testament. It helps to observe the overall patterns. The common idea in Paul's other uses of *noema* is the sum of a person's (or Satan's) thoughts rather than an individual thought. We tend to apply *"taking every thought captive"* the other way. The larger context of the book implies that Paul was referring to the place the false teachers had made for themselves in the Corinthian church. Notice, he speaks in the plural ("**we** *walk*," "**our** *warfare*"). The "we" doesn't mean every believer, because he says in verse 6, "**We** *are ready to punish all disobedience, when* **your** *obedience is complete*." Rather, Paul means he and his companions were going to take every competing ideology captive. The arena of battle, therefore, is what was being taught in the church. Even if a stronghold can be in the mind of an individual, this doesn't mean it is occupied by a demon. More likely the credit should be given to our flesh—that part of us that is not yet fully sanctified. Remember, spiritual warfare isn't aimed only at the devil, but at the world and flesh as well. We must learn to recognize the lies of the enemy that we have believed and replace them with the truth of God's Word.

I think we can all agree that strongholds are lies and wrong thinking. The indisputable solution is God's truth understood and applied. We may disagree about whether Satan can take control of an area of a believer's mind. I submit that the point of the passage is combating false teaching and wrong thinking in the church. Another application is that we need to recognize any wrong thinking we hold personally. If we study Scripture regularly, that ought to happen, for the Holy Spirit brings to mind those truths we need. We should employ the sword of the Spirit and the shield of the faith. I do not believe this passage teaches that wrong thinking means a demonic habitation in a believer.

BINDING THE DEVIL

Have you ever heard someone "bind" the devil in prayer? What about "binding" demons to bring some negative spiritual activity to a close? Have you ever done this? I have, but I must confess it didn't seem to change the circumstance. Since this week's lesson is focusing on our questions about certain spiritual warfare practices, let's ask a few regarding this one. Can I, as a follower of Christ, bind Satan and keep him from being able to work? Does every Christian have this authority? Hang on to your answer while we process the idea a bit. If these actions are part of our arsenal, why would we ever have to encounter an assault? If I can bind Satan, how is it that he always gets loose? If he has to stop at my word, what need is there to worry about such an impotent adversary? In this arena, as in every aspect of spiritual warfare, we must make sure our practice is supported in Scripture. It isn't enough to have a "proof-text" that we come up with to defend what we already believe. We must base our practice on the whole counsel of God's Word. Let's look at the biblical basis of this idea.

One place Scripture mentions the idea of "binding" is Matthew 12:29. Take a look at this verse and evaluate the surrounding context. It may also be helpful to compare the parallel accounts in Mark 3:27 and Luke 11:21–22.

Do you think the strong man is Satan?

_____

_____

_____

_____

Who binds this strong man?

_____

_____

_____

_____

Did You Know?

KEYS OF THE KINGDOM

To be in possession of the keys to a kingdom was the role of a doorkeeper. He was not the ruler of the city. He was one with delegated authority. He could only allow through the doors someone who met the criteria of the city authority. The key to the kingdom of heaven is the gospel, which is the power of God for salvation to those who believe. The New Testament does not show Peter exercising special authority that the other disciples did not possess.

Can a believer say, "I bind you, Satan," and control what he does and doesn't do? I certainly wish I had such authority. If I did, I would so bind Satan that he could never touch me, my family, my ministry, or anything on earth. In truth, however, only God has such authority, and He has chosen not to exercise it completely until the millennium (see Revelation 20:1–3). He does use His authority to set boundaries on Satan. Some attempt to limit Satan's actions against them or others by "binding the strong man," but this is not the point of the text. The roles here are obvious: the strong man is Satan, and Jesus is the *"someone stronger."* Matthew adds to this dialogue the statement, *"But if I cast out demons by the Spirit of God, then the kingdom of God has come upon you."* Jesus' subject seems to be our salvation. We were freed from the strong man so God could come in. The focus is not the absence of a demon, but the presence of the kingdom of God. It means nothing for the demon to leave, as Luke goes on to point out. If nothing takes its place, the demon is liable to come back and bring more with him. Our protection isn't a demon leaving, but the kingdom coming on us (at salvation).

Other places the idea of binding comes up in Scripture are Matthew 16:19 and 18:18.

APPLY What do you think the *"keys of the kingdom of heaven"* means?

_____

_____

_____

_____

Is this saying that heaven has to do what we say?

_____

_____

_____

_____

> "[Binding and loosing] is the church on earth carrying out heaven's decisions, not heaven ratifying the church's decision."
>
> (The New Linguistic and Exegetical Key to the Greek New Testament)

Questioning What Is Questionable

It is an appealing to think that we can make a decision and heaven will abide by it. But if this is what these passages are saying, where does God's sovereignty fit in? In context, this "binding and loosing" authority Peter is given relates to the gospel and to church discipline. The Greek construction here is very unique and difficult to convey accurately in English. I believe the Amplified Bible comes closest to capturing the meaning: *"Whatever you bind (declare to be improper and unlawful) on earth must be what is already bound in heaven; and whatever you loose (declare lawful) on earth must be what is already loosed in heaven."* Rather than giving Peter power, the declaration seems more focused on giving him accountability to align himself with God's will. Cleon Rogers offers this clarity: "It is the church on earth carrying out heaven's decisions, not heaven ratifying the church's decision."[3] The construction of the Greek grammar here (a perfect passive participle) literally translated would be *"shall be having been bound."* The perfect tense communicates that though the focus is future, the matter is already accomplished in the past. The passive voice makes clear we do *not* bind anything in heaven. The Bible as a whole refutes the idea that I can make heaven do anything. In addition, in neither of these passages does Jesus focus or limit this authority to the devil. The context seems to indicate it is to be used in sharing the gospel and in dealing with unrepentant sinners in the church.

REBUKING THE EVIL ONE

Can believers "rebuke" Satan and demons? If to "rebuke" means to command them to do our bidding, this concept offers great promise of victory in the Christian life. Jesus did some rebuking. He rebuked the wind and the sea (e.g. Matthew 8:26). He rebuked demons and cast them out of people (e.g. Matthew 17:18). He rebuked a woman's fever (Luke 4:39). He exercised His divine authority and made things obey Him. He also rebuked the disciples when they wanted to call down fire from heaven on the Samaritan village (Luke 9:55). I found that curious. If having the keys to the kingdom meant heaven would rubber stamp what they wanted, why were they reprimanded? It is of particular interest how Jesus responded when the disciples attempted rebuking. When Peter tried to rebuke Him for speaking of dying, Jesus strongly rejected this action (Matthew 16:22–23). Mark tells us Christ turned around and rebuked him back (Mark 8:33). When the disciples rebuked those who brought children for Jesus to lay hands on them, Jesus corrected them (Matthew 19:13–14). Mark's account relates, *"When Jesus saw this, He was indignant"* (Mark 10:14). The only place Jesus allowed them to rebuke was in confronting a sinning brother (Luke 17:3; see also 1 Timothy 5:20; 2 Timothy 4:2). Jesus' example of "rebuking" demons in the Gospels is not repeated by any of the apostles. It is a little hard today to identify the Scriptures people use to support this questionable practice. Does the Bible show the Enemy being rebuked by anyone other than the Lord?

📖 Look at 2 Peter 2:10–11, where the concept of people rebuking fallen celestial beings is addressed.

What does it mean to revile?

_____

_____

_____

What do you see implied in Peter saying *"they do not tremble"*?

_____

_____

_____

How does the example of angels contrast with the actions of those Peter is addressing?

_____

_____

_____

The Greek term translated *"revile"* here is *blasphemeo.* Our English word "blaspheme" is a transliteration of this expression. It means "to speak evil, to speak with impious irreverence concerning God Himself or what stands in some particular relation to Him."[4] The word itself carries the connotation of something that shouldn't be done and is always used negatively in Scripture. These people do what they shouldn't without even flinching. In stark contrast, Peter points to higher beings not behaving in such a manner. While the word "rebuke" is not used here, I believe the principle is relevant. A great many Christians speak flippantly about an angel who once held the highest position of that realm and served in the very presence of God. Yes, he is fallen, but judgment and vengeance belong only to the Lord. I take Peter's phrase *"they do not tremble"* as an admonition to think twice about how we speak of angels or to angels, even fallen ones.

The only Scripture to address anyone but the Lord rebuking the devil is Jude 1:8–10. The similarities between these verses and the passage from 2 Peter will be obvious. Peter spoke of what would soon take place in the church. Jude addresses it as currently happening. Examine this passage and let's ask some questions of it.

How are the actions of Michael contrasted with these men who *"revile angelic majesties"*?

_____

_____

_____

What position does Michael hold in heaven, and how does that relate?

_____

_____

_____

How does *"railing judgment"* relate to rebuking here?

_____

_____

_____

These men speak evil of all kinds of angels, while the highest angel refuses to do so of the chief rebel against God. If not even the *"archangel"* Michael (chief of the angels) can rebuke Satan, then I need to use caution myself. The wording here requires close scrutiny. The *"railing"* Michael avoids is the

---

A great many Christians speak flippantly about an angel who once held the highest position of that realm and served in the very presence of God.

Did You Know?

ARCHANGEL

"Archangel" is the first or highest rank of angel, a leader of the angels (See Daniel 10:13; 12:1). According to tradition, there are seven who stand immediately before the throne of God (Luke 1:19; Revelation 8:2), who have authority over other angels (Revelation 12:7). The only archangel definitely named is Michael (Daniel 10:13, 21; 12:1; Jude 1:9; Revelation 12:7). Some theologians believe Gabriel is also an archangel (Daniel 8:16; 9:21; Luke 1:19, 26). It is also argued that Satan was formerly an archangel before his fall. We do know he is a cherub, and scholars see implied in Ezekiel 28:12 that he was the chief angel.

Greek term *blasphemia*. Sound familiar? The root word is used yet again in verse 10. We are told that *"these men* revile *the things which they do not understand."* Clearly, Jude sees a close correlation between reviling and rebuking. A point from Greek grammar is worth adding. When Michael says *"the Lord rebuke you,"* the verb is in the optative mood. This mood is used to express a wish or desire. Michael is not telling the Lord to rebuke Satan. He is not even saying that He should. The archangel is expressing, "I hope he does!" Since there is no indication in Scripture that I, as a believer have such authority, and since the angels defer such practice to the Lord Himself, I have concluded that this is not an appropriate practice for me.

FOR ME TO FOLLOW GOD

We should be careful about seeking power. There is a seductive appeal to the idea of having special control over the demonic. What should our attitude be about casting out demons? The practice of some seems grossly inconsistent with Christ's admonition to the 70 after their evangelistic success. He warned, *"Do not rejoice in this, that the spirits are subject to you, but rejoice that your names are recorded in heaven"* (Luke 10:20). I shouldn't take joy in Satan's coming judgment. I should grieve over his rebellion and all who join him in it. Those who do encounter a demon as they seek to minister, and those who play a role in the departure of a demon, must recognize that this does not make them spiritually superior. Jesus made it clear that even unbelievers can cast out demons (see Matthew 7:22–23). Warfare is not a means of independence from God, but another aspect of our dependence upon Him. Therefore, prayer plays a prominent role in dealing with the devil.

One concern I have regarding some contemporary practice in spiritual warfare is a growing divergent view of prayer. Common to many prayer circles is a dependence on specifically worded prayers, as if saying the right incantation is the key. That idea has more in common with occultist spells than with Biblical Christianity. True prayer is simply talking to God. Since God knows our hearts, He will not ignore us for the lack of a formulaic invocation or because we mess up the wording. Dependence upon formula prayers places our trust in prayer rather than in God. There is nothing wrong with praying Scripture or with making certain that our request is doctrinally sound. However, prayer is simply a vehicle for communicating with the Lord and expressing our trust in Him. Our trust is in the One to whom we pray, not in how we pray.

Our trust is in the One to whom we pray, not in how we pray.

Allow me to tackle one additional question. Should believers pray for a "hedge of protection?" In Job 1:10 Satan alleges that God has made a *"hedge"* of protection *"around [Job]and his house and all that he has, on every side."* Think about the ramifications of Satan's statement. Where had he been? The devil says he had been *"roaming about on the earth and walking around on it"* (Job 1:7). How did he know that God's hedge covered Job on every side? Apparently he had walked the whole thing off, looking for an opening. As we have already discussed, God does set boundaries of protection around us, but there is no indication that Job had to pray for this. Job was unaware that the hedge existed until it was removed. Clearly, that hedge remains only so long as God wills it to, and Job's experience teaches us He sometimes removes it. This *"hedge"* of protection is a biblical reality, but it is not a promise I can claim or demand. The true role of prayer in spiritual warfare is keeping communication open with my commanding officer so He can guide me.

There is great danger in the pride that comes with thinking we have mastered spiritual warfare. James and Peter both begin their discussions of conflict with the devil by warning against pride. Both make the same statement: *"God is opposed to the proud, but gives grace to the humble"* (James 4:6; 1 Peter 5:5). Pride is rooted in self-sufficiency, self-control, and confidence in self, but God desires us to walk in dependence on Him. Could it be that pride in this area is a mark of one who is losing the battle rather than winning it? Was it not pride that caused Satan to be cast out of Heaven (see Isaiah 14:12–14)?

APPLY Consider this truth, and ask yourself if there are there any ways you struggle with pride in warfare?

_____

_____

_____

_____

_____

James 4:7–10 gives specific instructions on how we are to live out spiritual warfare through his series of eight imperatives. It is interesting indeed that of the eight actions he commands, only one even mentions the Devil. He places his primary focus squarely on how we relate to God. As we seek application this week, let's take time to evaluate our own living in light of James' directives.

Command #1: Submit to God
If we are submitted to God, it means that every area of our lives is yielded to His authority and control. Specific areas of sin are the consequence of the general offense of running our own lives. Why not take a moment to surrender your life afresh to the Lordship of Christ?

_____

_____

_____

_____

_____

Remember, the opposite of submission to God's will and way is following the promptings of our flesh, which is influenced by the world and the devil.

Command #2: Resist the Devil
As we studied in a previous lesson, resistance is all about standing firm rather than being drawn away. What are some areas where you find yourself being enticed by the devil?

James' Battle Plan:

- *Submit to God*
- *Resist the Devil (stand firm)*
- *Draw Near to God*
- *Cleanse Your Hands (actions)*
- *Purify Your Hearts (attitudes)*
- *Mourn Over Your Sin*
- *Humble Yourself*

_____

_____

_____

_____

_____

What actions have you taken to combat this?

_____

_____

_____

_____

_____

Command #3: Draw Near to God
Are you actively pursuing your relationship with God, or are you just going through the motions of church and religious activity?

_____

_____

_____

_____

_____

Battle Strategy:
Plan: _____
Place: _____
Priority: _____

Command #4: Cleanse Your Hands
The command to _"cleanse your hands"_ has to do with actions, while "purifying your heart" has to do with attitudes. Don't be introspective. Through prayer, invite the Holy Spirit to convict you of any actions in your life that are wrong. Confess those to the Lord (agree with Him that they are wrong), repent (turn from them), and yield that area of your life to Him. Use the space below to write this in prayer form.

_____

_____

_____

_____

_____

_____

Command #5: Purify Your Hearts
Are you aware of any attitudes in your heart that God has been putting His finger on? If so, deal with them as sin.

_____

_____

_____

_____

_____

_____

Command #6: Be Miserable

When James commands us to *"be miserable"* he isn't advocating "spiritual masochism," but just a more serious attitude about our sins. If there are any areas where you know you don't take your sin seriously, ask God to give you His heart toward this transgression.

_____

_____

_____

_____

_____

_____

_____

Command #7: Weep

Over what should you mourn and weep? The Greek word translated *"mourn"* here carries the idea of sorrow over sin. It correlates with #6. James makes the point twice to emphasize that we ought to feel about sin the way that God does. To "confess" (Gr. *homolegeo*) literally means "to agree." God wants us to have the same attitude about sin that He has.

Command #8: Humble Yourselves

As if to place bookends on his discussion of dealing with the devil, James ends where he began—humility. God constantly opposes the proud, but He continually pours out grace to the humble. We need to humble ourselves before God (which is the only logical attitude to have in light of His sovereign, omnipotent position). Our own exaltation must be left to His discretion and timing. All the other commands are summarized in the concept of humility before God. Why not close with a written prayer from a humble heart.

_____

_____

_____

_____

_____

_____

_____

_____

_____
_____
_____
_____
_____

1. Plato, as quoted by Adrian Woods and Paul Joyce in *Strategic Management: A fresh approach to developing skills, knowledge and creativity* (London: Kogan Page, 2001), 43.

2. "Strongholds," *GreatBibleStudy.com*, http://www.greatbiblestudy.com/strongholds.php.

3. Cleon L. Rogers Jr. and Cleon L. Rogers III, *The New Linguistic and Exegetical Key to the Greek New Testament* (Zondervan, 1998), 37.

4. Spiros Zodhiates, *The Complete Word Study Dictionary: New Testament* (Chattanooga: AMG Publishers, 1992), 340.

Notes

Notes

Notes

Notes

Notes

Notes

Notes

Made in United States
Orlando, FL
06 December 2021